# TO THE KING'S TASTE

# TO THE KING'S TASTE

Richard II's book of feasts and recipes *adapted for modern cooking by*

LORNA J. SASS

The Metropolitan Museum of Art

LIBRARY OF CONGRESS CATALOGING IN PUBLICATION DATA

Sass, Lorna J.
  To the King's taste.

  Original recipes from The Forme of cury interspersed in the text.
  Bibliography: p.
  Includes index.
  1. Cookery, English—Early works to 1800. 2. Great Britain—
History—Richard II, 1377–1399. I. The Forme of cury. II. Title.

TX705.S33                 641.5'942                 75–17859
ISBN 0–87099–133–7

# CONTENTS

Entrées, *continued*

## Side Dishes

## Sauces

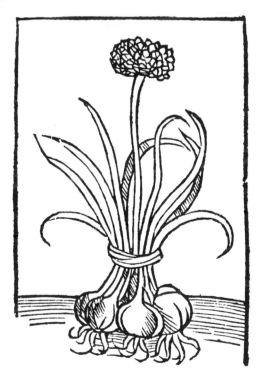

# PREFACE

**O**NE DAY a few years ago, while doing research for a paper on Chaucer in the stacks of Columbia University's library, I hesitated before the dark leather volumes published by the Early English Text Society. My eye fell upon a binding which read *Two Fifteenth Century Cookery Books*. Opening the book, I found that it contained a few hundred manuscript recipes written in Middle English. The language posed little difficulty, but many of the ingredients were unfamiliar, and the food combinations seemed quite unusual: salmon and fruit in a pie, elderflowers in cheesecake—nothing at all like the food I had eaten during a recent stay in England.

Next thing I knew, the book was propped up in my kitchen, and I was attempting to revive *tartee*, a pie with ground pork, raisins, prunes, *smale briddes*, and *pouder douce*. For *smale briddes*, I purchased two Cornish hens, but what was *pouder douce*? The recipe called for sugar, so I knew it wasn't that. . . .

An hour later, I sat at my table making a valiant effort to consume this concoction: bone dry, too many *smale briddes* and not enough pork, spices lost in an avalanche of raisins. I quickly realized that my life had been "measured out . . . with coffee spoons." Reared on the modern cookbook, I had never been challenged to develop my own sense of proportions.

By that time I had discovered that well over 90 percent of the ingredients were readily available, including the exotic spices. I had an intuitive feeling that the food, if properly prepared, would be quite unusual and delicious. And what better way to have "a taste" of the Middle Ages?

So I tested and retested the *tartee* recipe, each time learning from past mistakes, until I came out with a succulent, spicy pie which surprised and pleased both eye and taste buds. With this victory behind me, I felt impelled to bring back a cuisine that has been dead for more than four hundred years.

So here you are: medieval English cookery—sweet and spicy.

LORNA J. SASS

# INTRODUCTION

ALL BUT A FEW of the recipes in this book are from the *Forme of Cury* (Manner of Cookery), one of the earliest extant collections of manuscript recipes in Middle English. It was written about 1390 at the request of King Richard II, "the best and royallest viander of all Christian kings."[1] Many of the one hundred and ninety-six recipes in the *Forme of Cury* reveal the lust for grandeur and exoticism characteristic of Richard's court. Contemporary chroniclers report that the king feasted with more than ten thousand guests daily and employed three hundred cooks to prepare the royal repasts.

Richard's chefs were culinary artists. Some were sculptors, shaping enormous *sotelties* of colored marzipan to depict guests being honored at the feast. Others were architects, erecting towering castles of dough whose crenelated walls were actually the crusts of deep, stuffed pies:

> Take and make a foyle [leaf] of gode past with a roller, of a foot brode, and lynger by cumpas [in proportion]. Make foure coffyngs [pie crusts] of the self [same] past uppon the rolleres, the gretnesse of the smale of thyn arme, of six ynche deepnesse. Make the gretust in the myddel. Fasten the foile in the mouth upwarde, and fasten thee other foure in every side. Kerve out kyntlich [quaintly] kyrnels [crenelations] above in the manner of bataiwyng [embattlements] and drye hem harde in an ovene, other [or] in the sune. In the myddle coffyn do a fars [stuffing] of pork, with gode pork and ayren [eggs] rawe with salt, and color it with safron, and do in another creme of almandes, and helde [cast] it in another creme of cowe mylke with ayren. Color it with sandres [sandalwood]. Another manner. Fars of fyges, of raysons, of apples, of peeres, and hold it in bron [make it brown]. Another manner. Do fars as to frytors blanched [fried pastries stuffed with blanched, ground almonds], and

11

color it with grene. Put this to the ovene, and bake it wel, and serve it forth with ew ardant [hot water].

A few cooks became godlike creators, giving tangible form to the beasts of mythology. To make *cokentrice*, half capon and half pig, they instruct us to:

> Take a capoun, and skald hym, and draw hem clene, and smyte hem a-to [in two] in the waste overthwart [across the waist]. Take a pigge and skald hym, and draw hym in the same maner and smyte hem also in the waste. Take a nedyl and a threde, and sewe the fore partye of the capoun to the after parti of the pygge and the fore partye of the pigge to the hynder party of the capoun, and than stuffe hem as thou stuffyst a pigge. Putte hem on a spete and roste hym, and whan he is y-now [done], dore [make golden] hem with yolkys of eyroun [eggs] and pouder gynger and safroun, thenne wyth the ius [juice] of percely with-owte [on the outside], and than serve it forth for a ryal mete [royal food].

The most extravagant preparations were reserved for special feasts, but the cooks responded to creative impulses even when preparing ordinary fare. They particularly enjoyed coloring food, not to enhance natural beauty, but to disguise it.

All of the coloring agents were organic. The most popular was saffron, used to transform food to gold, the color traditionally associated with royalty. Like the *cokentrice*, many foods were sprinkled with parsley juice to dye them green. In the *Forme of Cury*, detailed instructions are given for preparing *lete lardes* (lard slices) by carefully layering portions of lard, each of which has been colored a different hue:

> Take parsel and grynde with a cowe mylk. Medle [mix] it with ayren [eggs] and lard ydyced [diced]. Take mylke after that thou hast done, and myng [mix] therewith, and make thereof diverse colours. If thou wolt [will] have yelow, do thereto safron, and no parsel. If thou wolt have it white, nonther [neither] parsel, ne safron, but do thereto amydon [fine wheat flour bleached in the sun]. If thou wilt have rede do thereto sandres [sandalwood]. If thou wilt have pownas [purple], do thereto turnesole [turnsole]. If thou wilt have blak, do thereto

blode ysode [boiled] and fryed. And set on the fyre in as many vessels as thou hast colours thereto, and seeth it wel, and lay thise colours in a cloth first oon [one] and sithen [then] another upon him, and sithen the thridde [third] and the ferthe, and presse it harde till it be all out clene. And whan it is all colde, lesh [slice] it thynne. Put it in a panne, and fry it wel, and serve it forth.

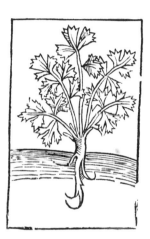

The scene of creativity, the medieval kitchen, was typically a separate structure of stone or brick about 30 feet square and 50 feet high. To accommodate the demands of a king like Richard, it had to have at least one fireplace large enough to roast whole oxen. In the center of the room, an open hearth raised on a plat-form of bricks supplemented cooking areas provided by fireplaces built into the walls.

The kitchen contained relatively little furniture. A large chopping block for smiting meat *on pecys* or into *gobettys* was essential, as was the *dressour*, a long massive plank on which food was given final embel-lishment before presentation in the great hall. Enor-mous mortars and pestles were in constant use for

13

pulverizing spices and pounding meats. There was often a large vat for storing freshly caught fish, and a locked spice cabinet.

Techniques of cookery were similar to our own. Even the cook in the *Canterbury Tales*, by no means an elegant chef, knew how to "roost and seeth and boille and frye." Manuscript recipes of the period recommend *parboyling, bakyng, stewyng, scaldyng, broylyng,* and *tostyng.*

Judging from menus, roasting was one of the most popular methods for preparing feast foods, perhaps because it required relatively little expert attention. In addition to whole oxen, haunches of venison, heads of boar, and game birds were turned on spits by broach turners hired especially for the royal repasts.

Roasting flesh was frequently basted with a paste of saffron, egg yolks, and flour to give it a gilded appearance. By this *endoring* process, pork balls were transformed into *pomes dorryle*, golden apples (recipe, p. 82). Endoring is also suggested in the preparation of peacocks for a *Feste Roiall*:

> Take and flee off the skynne with the fedurs, tayle, and the nekke, and the head theron [leaving the head on]. Then take the skyn with all the fedurs and lay hit on a table abrode [spread out] and strawe [sprinkle] theron grounded comyn [cumin]. Then take the pecokke, and roste hym, and endore hym with rawe yolkes of egges, and when he is rosted take hym of [off the spit] and let hym coole awhile, and take and sowe [sew] hym in his skyn, and gilde his combe, and so serve hym forthe with the last cours.

The peacock came to a more magnificent end than most animals which were traditionally slaughtered and salted in the late fall. Any fat, plump carcass "worth its salt" would be preserved, either by burial in a granular bed of salt or by immersion in a strong solution of salt and water.

Since there was no refrigeration, salted meats were often the only flesh available. As a result, many medieval recipes advise boiling the meat to soften it before proceeding with further preparations. The fourteenth-century Goodman of Paris instructs his young wife on the subject:

> The haunch which is salted ought to be cooked first in water and wine to get rid of the salt, and then throw away the wine and water and afterwards set it to cook slowly in the meat broth and turnips, and serve it in strips with water in a dish.[2]

For boiling and stewing, massive cauldrons reaching to men's waists stood on three legs directly over the flames. "Seeth it stondyng," the *Forme of Cury* frequently advises: "Cook it thick." Chaucer's cook seethes one of his specialties, *mortrewes*, a thick paste of ground meat, eggs, and bread crumbs equivalent in texture to pâté. To make *mortrewes*:

> Take hennes and pork and seeth hem togydre. Take the lyre [flesh] of hennes and of the pork and hewe it small, and grinde it all to doust. Take brede ygrated and do [add] thereto, and temper [mix] it with the salf [same] broth and alye [combine] it with yolks of ayren [eggs] and cast thereon powder-fort [strong spice]. Boile it and do therein powder of gynger, sugar, safronn, and salt and loke that it be stondyng [thick] and floer [sprinkle] it with powdor gynger.

Although frequently mentioned in literature and manuscript recipes of the period, *mortrewes* is never found on feast menus. It is the perfect leftovers dish, an excellent preparation for making old meat palatable.

While large quantities of food would be cooked directly in the iron cauldrons, smaller amounts were placed in earthenware jars with watertight lids. These jars were immersed into a cauldron of boiling water and set to rest on a shelf pierced with holes which fit across the cauldron about three-quarters of the way down.

In many recipes, Richard's cooks order us to "frye it uppe in gode grece." Butter or *whyte grece* (lard) was melted in frying pans much the shape of our own except for their exceptionally long handles. These pans were rested on round iron frames which hung from the rafters; heat intensity was modified by raising or lowering the frames. A favorite fried food was *fritors* (fritters) of apples or parsnips (recipe, p. 84). The fruit or vegetable slices were dipped into a foamy batter of ale, eggs, and flour, and fried to golden brown.

When not in use, utensils were hung from hooks or stored on shelves along the kitchen walls. All utensils had long handles so that the cooks could stand a safe distance from the flames. In one manuscript picture, the handle of a basting ladle is so long that it can be made to reach across the length of a spit on which four boars are roasting. In fact, the shaft appears to be about one and a half times the height of the boy holding it.

A three-pronged flesh hook was used for drawing seething carcasses out of the cauldrons. *Skymours* (slotted spatulas) were employed to skim off grease and to remove fried foods from the pan. *Straynours* were required to purée solids and to make bread crumbs of crusts. When eggs were pushed through them repeatedly, strainers performed the function of egg beaters.

The kitchen had at least one large oven for baking the various custards, pies, and pastries generically called *bake metes* (baked foods). The oven was generally oval-shaped and built into the thickness of the kitchen wall. To prepare it for use, a bundle of faggots was placed inside and lighted, and an iron door closed in front. Once the faggots had burned, making the air inside the oven and all the surrounding brickwork very hot, the door was opened. The ashes were quickly swept out and the pastries shoved within. The door was closed, and the *bake metes* cooked as the oven cooled.

In the larger households, breads were prepared in bakehouses, separate structures with ovens sometimes as wide as 14 feet. Aside from the fine-quality round loaves served for eating at the feast (recipe, p. 113), bakers were responsible for preparing trencher loaves. These were made of coarser grains and cut in half horizontally to serve as bread plates after they had been left to harden for four days.

The following instructions, translated from a fourteenth-century source, explain the preparation of *manchet* loaves, a fine-quality bread:

> First your meal, ground and bolted through the finest cloth, you shall put into a clean kimmel [kneading tub] and, opening the flour hollow in the middle, put into it the best ale barme, three pints to a bushel of meal, and some salt to season it with. Then put in your liquor [liquid] reasonably warm and knead it through the brake [dough hook] or put it in a cloth and with your feet tread it a good space together. Then let it lie an hour so as to swell. Take it forth and mould it into manchets, round and flat. Score it about the waist to give it leave to rise, and prick it with your knife on the top, and so put it into your oven and bake it with gentle heat.[3]

A popular bread dish in the Middle Ages was *rastons* (stuffed bread loaves; recipe, p. 114). After the top crust was carefully cut away, the soft inner part was scooped out, crumbled, and fried in mutton fat or butter. Often salt, cinnamon, mace, and raisins were added. Then the stuffing was replaced in the bread shell and the top put back in place. The loaf was rewarmed before serving.

## Fowl, Meat, and Fish

The quantity and assortment of fowl available to the medieval nobleman are impressive. The *Forme of Cury* has recipes for hen, capon (recipe, p. 67), partridge, curlew, pigeon, *smale briddes* (recipe, p. 54), cranes, heron, duck, goose (recipe, p. 56), and chicken (recipes, pp. 68, 71). Feast menus of the period also include roasted quail, lark, bittern, plover, rail, dove, cygnet, peacock, egret, woodcock, snipe, dotterel, gull, and teal. Most often fowl was roasted and endored, but for some feasts it was stewed in thick, spicy sauce or teased into small pieces and served with rice (recipe, p. 71).

Rabbit was popular fare, and it was often cooked and served in a highly spiced sauce (recipe, p. 53). Roasted oxen, mutton, beef, kid, deer, and pork were sliced by the carver and served with pungent, vinegar-based sauces. Boiled pork was often ground and combined with spices to stuff a pie (recipe, p. 54), or encased in pastry shells for *tartlettes* (recipe, p. 36).

On meatless Lenten days, feast menus included primarily fish. The list of available seafood is lengthy, particularly for coastal areas. The *Forme of Cury* mentions porpoise, haddock, codling, hake, salmon, tench, pike, eel, turbot, plaice, roach, rayfish, mackerel, gurnard, oysters, mussels, and lampreys. Other contemporary recipe sources include bream, flounder, gudgeon, marling, halibut, whelks, perch, sturgeon, trout, crab, and carp. Salted herrings and dried stockfish (generally cod), imported from the Baltic and North seas, were staples for the winter months. Fish was fried, served with a spicy sauce (recipe, p. 61), baked in a pie (recipe, p. 62), boiled in a stew (recipe, p. 41), or prepared in aspic (recipe, p. 46).

For the great feast on September 23, 1387, given by King Richard and the Duke of Lancaster, the cooks gathered the following provisions:

14 oxen lying in salte
2 oxen ffreyssh
120 hedes of shepe fressh
120 carcas of shepe fressh
12 bores
14 calvys
140 pigges
300 maribones
of larde and grece, ynogh [enough]
3 ton of salt veneson
3 does of ffressh veneson
50 swannes
210 gees
50 capons of hie grece [larded]
8 dozen other capons
60 dussen hennes
400 conyngges [large rabbits]
4 fesauntes
5 herons and bitores
6 kiddes
5 dozen pullayn for gely [pullets for jelly]
12 dozen to roast
100 dozen peions [pigeons]

12 dozen partrych [partridges]
 8 dozen rabettes
12 dosen curlewes
12 cranes
wilde fowle ynogh
120 galons melke
12 galons creme
11 galons of cruddes [curds]
12 bushels of appelles
11 thousand egges

There is no account of the number of guests invited. Ten thousand, perhaps?

### Herbs, Flowers, and Vegetables

"What is an herb?" the eighth-century Alcuin inquired of Charlemagne. "The friend of physicians and the praise of cooks," the emperor replied. The medicinal and culinary values of herbs were highly regarded in the Middle Ages. "There is no Herbe nor weede but god hath gyven vertue them to helpe man," states the sixteenth-century Doctor of Physick Andrew Boorde.[4]

*Erbolate* (recipe, p. 78), a baked egg dish with herbs, was an extremely wholesome preparation. Dr. Boorde comments on the medicinal values of some of the herbs included:

20

Parsley is good to breke the stone and causeth a man to pysse; it is good for the stomacke, and doth cause a man to have a swete breth. . . . Isope [hyssop] clenseth viscus fleume [phlegm], and is good for the breste and for the lunges. . . . Sawge is good to help a woman to conceyve and doth provoke uryne. . . . Fennell-sede is used to breke wynde and good agaynst poyson.

Few herbs aside from saffron are listed in the household accounts among purchases, primarily because almost everything needed was taken from the castle garden. A rhyming treatise of the fifteenth century written by "Mayster Ion Gardener" instructs the gardener:

> How he schall hys sedys [seeds] sowe.
> Of every moneth he most knowe
> Bothe of wortys [cabbages] and of leke [leek]
> Ownyns [onions] and of garleke
> Percely, clarey and eke [also] sage
> And all other herbage [plants]. . . .[5]

In the Middle Ages no distinction was made among herbs, flowers, and vegetables; all were considered parts of growing plants. Among the seventy *herbys* mentioned in the treatise are pellitory, rue, dittany, sage, clary, thyme, hyssop, orach, mints, savory, spinach, lettuce, avens, borage, fennel, southernwood, wormwood, vervain, chamomile, leek, radish, rose, and St.-John's-wort. Another treatise of the period gives a list of salad herbs (recipe, p. 80): violets, parsley, red mints, watercress, purslane, rosebuds, daisies, dandelions, rocket, red nettle, borage flowers, red fennel, chickweed, and ramson.[6] Flowers were used not only in salads, but as the primary flavoring agent in many rich desserts (recipes, pp. 100, 103).

Ion Gardener gives special instruction on the nature of saffron, one of the most popular medieval culinary herbs. He tells us that the crocus bulb should be planted at least three inches deep in beds of dung during September. Although most saffron was imported, it was grown in some of the eastern counties of England, and the plant gave its name to the town of Saffron Walden in Essex. Since it takes the stigmas of seventy-five thousand crocus flowers to make one pound of saffron, the price always remained extremely high.

Although vegetables were not considered worthy of feast fare, the high percentage of recipes for preparing them given in the *Forme of Cury* demonstrates that they were often eaten in the household. Root vegetables such as parsnips (recipe, p. 84), turnips, radishes, and skirrets were particularly common, perhaps due to their long growing season. Popular, too, were the favorites of Chaucer's Summoner: garlic, onions, and leek. Cabbages, peas (recipe, p. 45), beans, beets, squash (recipe, p. 42), and mushrooms (recipe, p. 76) were all available to provide a considerably varied vegetable diet.

*Spices*

The vast array of spices that grew in China, Java, and along the Malabar Coast of India reached England via Venetian merchants who purchased them primarily in Alexandria. The Arabs monopolized the spice trade, guarding their secret sources so carefully that Western Europe did not discover them until the late fifteenth century. One explanation for the mysterious origin of spices was given by Joinville, a chronicler of the Crusades:

> Before the river [Nile] enters into Egypt, people who are accustomed so to do, cast their nets out-spread into the river at night and when morning comes, they find in their nets such goods as are sold by weight and brought into the land: ginger, rhubarb, wood of aloes, and cinnamon. And it is said that these things come from the earthly paradise, just as the wind blows down the dry wood in the forests of our own land. The dry wood of the trees in paradise that thus falls into the river is sold to us by the merchants.[7]

Despite their high price, spices were considered an

"essential luxury." No household account among the nobility lacks its long list of purchased spices. Whole spices were generally pulverized with a mortar and pestle, and the large households employed yeoman powderbeaters for just this purpose. Ground spices are referred to as *pouders* in the recipes, and a distinction is made between *whyte pouder* (ginger or a combination of ginger or mace with confectioner's sugar), *pouder fort* (ginger or a blend of cinnamon and mace), and *pouder douce* (one or more of the sweet spices: anise, fennel, and nutmeg).

Pepper was one of the most highly prized spices during the period, perhaps because of the strong belief in its digestive qualities. Legend has it that when the eighth-century English cleric Bede approached his death, he distributed his few treasures among the brethren and divided a little parcel of pepper as one of his choicest possessions.

Bartholomew the Englishman, the lively thirteenth-century encyclopedist, had a very interesting explanation for the different varieties of pepper:

Pepper is the seed of the fruit of a tree that groweth in the south side of the hill Caucases, in the strong heat of the sun. And serpents keep the woods that pepper groweth in. And when the woods of pepper are ripe, men of that country set them on fire, and chase away the serpents by violence of fire. And by such burning the grain of pepper that was white by nature is made black.[8]

The guild of Pepperers, organized in the eleventh century, was early in the fourteenth century given charge of the *peso grosso*, the heavy beam used to weigh spices by the pound. Guild members came to be called *grossarii*, the probable ancestor of our word "grocer."

Ginger, thought to "quycken the remembraunce," was a popular spice in the medieval kitchen, and various types were known: green, white, columbine, and string, among others. The accounts are scant and confusing, but it seems that green ginger was young and just ripe, therefore quite juicy and mild. White ginger was probably the partially dried root with which we are more familiar. The Goodman of Paris advises his wife on the relative value of string and columbine ginger: "String ginger has a darker skin and is softer to the knife to cut, and lighter inside than the other . . . better and always dearer."

Another praised aromatic root was galingale. It is related to the ginger family, but its taste is rather bitter. Galingale root was pulverized and used in the preparation of a sauce called *galyntyne* (recipe, p. 90) which accompanied meat, fowl, or fish.

An unusual whole spice used in medieval cookery is the cubeb. A little berry from Java, it tastes like a cross between allspice and peppercorn. Cubeb has a pungent, aromatic flavor and makes a tangy contribution to sauces of all kinds. Another pepperlike berry, although smaller and teardrop-shaped, is the grain of paradise (sometimes called grain of Paris). *Greyns* were thought to be good for the stomach and head and soothing to the throat. Belief in the efficacy of this

24

healer from paradise was held by Chaucer's Prioress, who recounts the story of a murdered child who begins to sing when Mary places a *greyn* upon his tongue.

Other commonly used spices were clove and cinnamon, often called *gilofre* and *canel*. Less prevalent, although certainly known, were cardamom, cumin, and coriander.

In addition to being used in cookery, whole spices were often served as digestive agents at the end of the feast, either plain or in confection.

As a rule, possibly because of its importation from the East, sugar was classified as a spice. Sugar was generally sold in a loaf, the most prized being *sugre cypre* (sugar of Cyprus). There were also *blake sugre* (brown sugar) and *pouder sugre* (confectioner's). Since most households kept their own beehives, honey, the other popular sweetener, was rarely purchased.

## Fruits

Although a considerable variety of fruit was available in medieval England, doctors felt that raw fruit was extremely difficult to digest. As a result, most fruits were cooked in sugary syrups and pies or fermented into ciders.

The fruits most frequently mentioned in the recipes are Warden pears, bullace and damson plums, medlars, quinces, blaunderelles, apples, grapes, cherries, mulberries, strawberries, and pomegranates. Peaches were apparently available, but were of an inferior quality. Oranges and lemons were imported from Portugal and the Levant, as were large quantities of dried fruits such as raisins, currants (the name is derived from the Middle English *raisens of Corinth*), prunes, dates, and figs.

If fruit was served raw after the meal, it was preferably to be accompanied by foods which aided the digestion: *ypocras*, hard cheese, nuts, and confectioned spices.

## Wines and Other Drinks

Strength and harshness were the qualities most characteristic of medieval wines. Since glass bottles were unknown and the proper treatment of wine in casks only imperfectly understood, wines had to be consumed within a year of the harvest, before they turned to vinegar.[9]

Although a small amount of wine was produced in southern England, the great majority was imported from the vineyards of Gascony, the Rhine, and Moselle. The grapes were generally harvested and pressed in September, and the resultant *must*, the unfermented juice of the mature grape, was stored in wooden casks. As soon as fermentation began and the initial scum was removed, some casks were sealed for shipping as *wine of vintage*. Other casks were sealed, racked for six to eight months, and exported in the spring as *wine of rec.* The latter, clearer and more delicate than *wine of vintage*, was considered preferable and brought a higher price.

The wide variety of wine drunk at the feast table and used in cookery is indicated by a list in the fifteenth-century treatise called the *Boke of Kervyng*

(Carving).[10] Mention is made of red and white wines as well as numerous varieties of sweet wine imported from Greece, Italy, Portugal, and Spain.

Many of the recipes call for *gode wyne* (wine of good quality), or specifically for *wyne greke* (Greek wine). The term *wyne greke* did not necessarily designate the origin of the wine, but that it was made after the style of either Greek or Cyprus wine. Such wines were generally made in Pouille and Calabria and were heavy and sweet.

By adding honey, herbs, or spices, attempts were made to disguise the natural harshness and acidity of improperly aged wines. Such blends were known as *piments*, named for the *pigmentarii* or apothecaries who recommended them as medicinal cures. *Ypocras* (recipe, p. 122), a red or white wine infused with various aromatic ingredients, was the most popular *piment*. Named for Hippocrates, *ypocras* was thought to be a salutary and digestive drink.

In fact, moderate consumption of all wine was considered beneficial to the health. Dr. Boorde tells us that it "doth quycken a man wyttes; it doth comfort the hert; it doth scowre [scour] the lyver, and it doth ingender gode blode." In another medical treatise, we are told that *soppes in wyne*, the favorite medieval breakfast of bread soaked in wine, "purges the teeth and sharpens the sight, for it lets the evil fumes ascend to the brain; it digests perfectly meats not well digested."[11]

Ale was also a popular drink, particularly in the summer months, by which time most of the wine had turned to vinegar. Says Dr. Boorde, "Ale for an Englysshe man is a naturall drynke. Ale must have these propertyes: it must be fresshe and cleare, it muste not be ropy nor smoky." Ale was made of barley, corn, or oats, either singly or in combination. Since hops were regarded with suspicion as dangerous to the health, beer did not become a popular drink in England until the sixteenth century.

Many drinks were made from the fermented juices of fruits: *cyder* from apples, *perry* from pears, *raspes* from raspberries. When juices became too fermented to be drunk, they were used as vinegar in cookery.

The scene of the feast was the castle's great hall, an enclosed room measuring perhaps 100 feet long, 45 feet wide, and 60 feet high. A raised platform ran the width of the room; on it stood the *high borde* or dais at which the king and honored guests dined. Subordinate tables paralleled the side walls to accommodate less distinguished trenchermen.

In the room's center, a huge fire blazed. To keep chilly drafts to a minimum, decorative tapestries were hung on all the walls, the most majestic providing a backdrop for the high borde.

Since all of the castle's social activity took place in the great hall, tables made of long wooden planks balanced on trestles were set up especially for mealtime and dismantled immediately thereafter. The king had a special chair with back, arms, and cushions, while the guests sat on *banquettes*, the small backless benches which have given their name to the feast itself.

The room was sparsely furnished. There was a long sideboard on which cooked food, wine, and goblets were set to rest before being served. A large decorative screen shielded the passageway to the kitchen. Above it, a minstrels' gallery jutted out from its 10-foot-high perch on the wall.

*It is ten thirty, about a half hour before dinner is to be served. The marshal raises his rod in the sunlit hall and commands the* ewerer *(who takes charge of the water basin or* ewery*) to set three linen cloths on the high borde. These are stretched and placed on the king's table with elaborate ceremony.*

*Meanwhile, ushers and grooms arrange subordinate tables with cloths, napkins, and* surnapes *(special towels used for drying hands after they are washed between courses of the meal). At each setting, the ushers place a trencher, a mazer cup, and a spoon.*[12]

Small round loaves of fine-quality bread are strewn in no seeming pattern about the table.

Suddenly clarions echo throughout the hall announcing the arrival of the king and honored guests. As they are seated, the pantner (responsible for serving pan, bread) drapes a towel around his neck and over his shoulders so that he holds an end in each of his hands. On an outstretched left arm, he balances the sovereign's napkin, seven loaves of eating bread, and four trencher loaves; in the left hand he carries the principal saltcellar for the king's table. He then approaches the high borde, and with the help of the ewerer and butler (named for boteilles, the wine bottles stored under his supervision), places the salt to the king's right and the trenchers to his left. He puts two carving knives haft outwards before the carver and sets the third down haft inwards before the lord. The pantner then takes his own three special knives and prepares the bread plates from round trencher loaves by cutting off the top crust, and squaring and smoothing off the edges of the bottom one. The king will eat from one such trencher; the carver will use the other three as cutting boards for meat.

The pantner now kneels before the king, and the carver cuts him a slice of bread from the high-quality loaf to be assayed. As the pantner rises, the elaborate hand-washing ceremony begins.

The ewerer approaches the dais with two basins. He strains the water from one through a cloth folded "with fulle grete lore" (with great learning) into another. He then pours some of the water into a cup of white wood and tastes it, after re-covering the basin with the cloth.

The carver now takes both basins. A squire or a knight removes the towel, and the carver pours more of the water into a cup and drinks. Now that the water has been sufficiently tested, the king may use what is left for washing his hands.

As the Latin grace is chanted in unison, a procession of trusted servants emerges from the kitchen, each carrying a resplendent creation prepared by the chefs. Hidden under ornate silver covers are the multitude of delicacies that Richard will sample on this day, September 23, 1387:

THE FIRST COURSE

Venison with furmenty (sliced venison in a sauce of boiled, hulled wheat)

A potage called Viaundbruse (a broth made of choice meats)

Hedes of Bores

Grete Flessh (roasted haunches of meat)

Swannes rosted

Pigges rosted
Crustade Lumbard in paste (custard with dried fruit,
   parsley, and bone marrow baked in a crust;
   recipe, p. 104)
And a Sotelte

THE SECONDE COURSE
A potage called Gele (jellied soup)
A potage de Blandesore (capon or hen cooked in a
   broth of almond milk, spiced with ginger, mace, and
   cubebs, and thickened with rice flour)
Pigges rosted
Cranes rosted
Fesauntes rosted
Herons rosted
Chekens endored
Breme (bream)
Tartes
Broke braune (carved flesh)
Conyngges rosted (roasted rabbits)
And a Sotelte

THE THIRDE COURSE
Potage. Bruete of Almonds (almond soup)
Stwde Lumbarde (a stew prepared in the style of
   Lombardy)
Venyson rosted
Chekenes rosted
Rabettes rosted
Quailes rosted
Larkes rosted
Payne puff (egg yolks, bone marrow, dates, raisins, and
   ginger baked in a pie crust)
A dissh of gely
Longe Frutours (curds, eggs, and flour fried and cut
   into small pieces with sugar sprinkled on top just
   before serving)
And a Sotelte

*The feast lasts as long as the daylight. Just as the
sun begins to fade, the cupbearer serves goblets of
ypocras and wafers. The pantner places trays of whole
spices in confection on each table. After a few moments King Richard rises and bids farewell to his
guests. Healthful digestion and a good night's rest are
now the primary concerns.*

1. This description of Richard is given by the cooks at the beginning of the *Forme of Cury*.

2. Eileen Power, trans., *Goodman of Paris* (London, 1928), p. 250. The turnips would aid in drawing salt from the meat.

3. Dorothy Hartley, *Food in England* (London, 1954), p. 509. Unfortunately the original source is not given.

4. This and other quotes of Dr. Boorde are taken from the *Dyetary*, ed. F. J. Furnivall (London, 1870), *passim*.

5. Alicia Amherst, ed., "A Fifteenth Century Treatise on Gardening by 'Mayster Ion Gardener,'" *Archaeologia*, 54 (1844), 160.

6. From Sloane Manuscript 1201. Reproduced in Alicia Amherst, *A History of Gardening in England* (London, 1896), pp. 75–76.

7. Margaret Labarge, *A Baronial Household of the Thirteenth Century* (New York, 1965), p. 88.

8. Robert Steele, *Medieval Lore from Bartholomaeus Anglicus* (London, 1907), p. 108.

9. This discussion of wine is taken primarily from André Simon, *The History of the Wine Trade in England*, Vol. I (London, 1906), *passim*.

10. See F. J. Furnivall, *Early English Meals and Manners* (London, 1868), pp. 151–74.

11. Quoted in William Mead, *The English Medieval Feast* (New York, 1967), p. 128.

12. The fork was not used at table in England until the seventeenth century, and each guest customarily brought his own knife.

# Recipes

In the Middle English recipes which follow, punctuation has been added to facilitate reading, but characteristic irregularities of spelling have been maintained. Although translations are literal in meaning, word order has occasionally been altered to coincide with contemporary English usage.

For the convenience of the modern reader, the recipes have been divided into sections on appetizers, entrées, side dishes, sauces, desserts, and miscellaneous. These classifications were not made in the Middle Ages, as you can detect from glancing at the menu for Richard's feast (p. 31), and many of the recipes would fall comfortably under two or more categories.

The tested recipes with suggested quantities are offered as guidelines for your own creative efforts. In my interpretations I have followed the medieval instructions whenever possible, but in favor of the most pleasing taste and texture, I have departed from the original instructions at times. For example, when I boiled the rabbit for *Connynges in Cyrip*, I found the meat to be tough and tasteless. So I recommend browning it in seasoned flour. In the case of the sauces —which are all vinegar-based—I have tempered the acidity by the addition of stock. My aim has been to find a common meeting ground for the medieval palate and our own, and the recipes have been chosen and developed with that goal in mind.

BON APPÉTIT

# appetizers

*Tartlettes* Take pork ysode and grynde it small with safronn. Medle it with ayren and raisons of coraunce and powdor fort and salt, and make a foile of dowhg and close the fars there-inne. Cast the tartletes in a panne with faire water boillyng and salt. Take of the clene flessh withoute ayren, and boile it in gode broth. Cast thereto powdor-douce and salt, and messe the tartletes in disshes and helde the sewe thereonne.

*Little Tarts* Take cooked pork and grind it small with saffron. Mix it with eggs, currants, strong powder, and salt. Make a thin leaf of dough and enclose the stuffing in it. Cast the tartlettes in a pan of boiling salted water. Take some un-spiced meat without eggs, and boil it in good broth. Add sweet powder and salt. Divide the tartlettes into portions in dishes and pour the broth on top.

# LiTTLE TARTS

Making homemade noodle dough takes some elbow grease, but taste rewards effort. The "won tons" are stuffed with spiced pork and currants, and make an unusual highlight for a simple broth.

FOR NOODLE DOUGH
**2 cups sifted flour**
**$1/_2$ teaspoon salt**
**1 egg, lightly beaten**
**about $1/_4$ cup cold water**

1. Sift flour and salt together.
2. Make a small well in the center of the flour, and pour egg and water into it.
3. Combine all ingredients, mixing and kneading until a smooth, elastic dough is formed (about 10 minutes).
4. Allow dough to sit for about 20 minutes.
5. Divide dough in half. On a lightly floured surface, roll out halves one at a time into sheets almost paper thin. Dough will be elastic, and much de-termination is required in this process. Your task

will be eased by allowing a section of the dough leaf to hang over the table's side as you roll.

6. Cut each sheet of dough into about 10 or 12 rectangular pieces.

FOR FILLING AND BROTH
3 eggs
1/8 teaspoon saffron
1/4 teaspoon cinnamon
pinch mace
10 cubebs, finely crushed
1/4 teaspoon aniseed
1/8 teaspoon each cloves and nutmeg
1/2 teaspoon salt
3/4 pound ground pork
1/3 cup currants
6 cups chicken or beef stock

1. Beat 2 eggs, spices, and salt together.
2. Blend egg mixture, pork, and currants.
3. Place a teaspoon of stuffing on each piece of dough.
4. Beat the third egg. Run this "paste" along the edges of each piece of dough. Fold dough over stuffing so edges meet. Seal by pressing edges together.
5. Bring stock to boil. Add tartlettes and any leftover stuffing, reducing heat to a gentle boil.
6. Cook about 10 to 12 minutes or until noodle dough reaches consistency you enjoy in spaghetti.

SERVES 6

**The leve [dear] lorde . . . ete a sop hastyly, when he hade herde masse.**

*Sir Gawain and the Green Knight* (c. 1360)

*Slete Soppes* Take white of leeks and slyt hem and do hem to seeth in wyne, oile and salt. Rost brede and lay in dysshes and the sewe above and serve it forth.

*Slit Sops* Take the white of leeks and slit them. Boil them in wine, oil, and salt. Toast bread and place it in dishes with the stew above, and serve it forth.

# slit sops

The leek was a popular vegetable in the Middle Ages, perhaps because of the belief that it stimulated the appetite. But leek also had its harmful effects: "It causes headache and gives bad dreams . . . after eating it, some lettuce, purslane, or endive should be taken, to temper its heating effects."*

What follows is a medieval cousin to vichyssoise.

> 4 medium leeks
> 2 tablespoons butter
> 1½ cups dry white wine *or* 1 cup canned consommé plus ½ cup wine
> ¼ teaspoon salt
> freshly ground pepper
> beurre manié: 2 tablespoons flour blended with 1 tablespoon soft butter
> sops: 1–2 slices toast, quartered, *or* ½ cup croutons

1. Remove green tops and roots of leeks. Cut white section in half lengthwise and once across the middle. Wash thoroughly.
2. Melt butter in a heavy saucepan. Toss leeks to coat, and sauté over a gentle flame until they begin to wilt (about 5 minutes).
3. Add wine, salt, and pepper to taste. Simmer an additional 10 to 15 minutes until leeks are done.
4. Blend in beurre manié to thicken just before serving.
5. Serve in soup bowls over toast or croutons.

SERVES 2

---

* Arthur Way, trans., *The Science of Dining: A Medieval Treatise on the Hygiene of the Table* (London, 1936), p. 29.

A ferthyng-worth of muscles were a feste for suche folke.

LANGLAND
*Piers Plowman's Creed* (1393)

*Muskels in Brewet*  Take muskels, pyke hem, seeth hem with the owne broth. Make a lyor of crustes and vynegar; do in oynon mynced, and cast the muskels thereto, and seeth it, and do thereto powdor with a lytel salt and saffron. The samewise make of oysters.

*Mussels in Broth*  Take mussels and pick them over. Boil them in their own broth. Make a thickener of bread crusts and vinegar. Add minced onions and then the mussels. Cook it, adding some spices, a little salt, and saffron. Prepare oysters in the same way.

# mussels in broth

Here is a pungent ancestor of *moules marinière*:

3 pounds mussels, scrubbed and bearded
3 cups boiling water
1 large onion, minced
3 cloves garlic, minced
2 tablespoons butter
3 tablespoons finely ground bread crusts
2 teaspoons (or more) vinegar
salt to taste
$^1/_2$ teaspoon saffron
$^1/_8$ teaspoon freshly ground pepper or cubeb
garnish: minced fresh parsley

1. Plunge mussels into boiling water. Cover and
   cook over high flame just until shells open
   (less than a minute).
2. Remove cooked mussels with a slotted spoon.
   Strain broth through fine mesh strainer.
3. Meanwhile, sauté onion and garlic in butter in a
   heavy skillet until onion is transparent.
4. Return broth to a pan. Add onion and garlic,
   bread crusts, vinegar, salt, saffron, and pepper
   or cubeb. Simmer, stirring until smooth and well
   blended. Check seasoning.
5. Remove mussels from shells and add them to the
   broth.
6. Cover and simmer about 15 seconds.
7. Serve in soup bowls, garnished with parsley.

SERVES 4

He behelde a fruyt fyzt feire and swete
"Gourdes" thus men clepe [called] the name.

ROBERT MANNING OF BRUNNE
*Handlyng Synne* (1303)

*Gourdes in Potage*  Take young gowrdes, pare hem, and kerve hem on pecys. Cast hem in gode broth and do thereto a good partye of oynonns mynced. Take pork soden. Grynde it, and alye it therewith and with yolkes of ayren. Do thereto safronn and salt and messe it forth with powdor-douce.

*Gourd Soup*  Take young gourds. Pare them and carve them into pieces. Cast them into good broth, adding a good portion of minced onions. Take cooked pork, grind it, and mix it with egg yolks. Add saffron and salt and serve it forth with sweet powder.

# GOURD SOUP

Gerard explains: "There are divers sorts of Gourds, some wilde, others tame of the garden: some bearing fruit like unto a bottle; others long, bigger at the end, keeping no certain form or fashion; some greater, others lesse."* Perhaps young gourds are those with soft skins, like cucumber and zucchini. But the soup is also exciting with pumpkin (varieties of which almost certainly existed in the Middle Ages), or butternut squash (a product of the New World).

$^1/_2$ **pound ground pork**
$^1/_2$ **teaspoon salt**
**2 large onions, minced**
**2 tablespoons butter**
**6 cups vegetable or chicken stock**
$^1/_2$ **teaspoon minced fresh ginger**
$^1/_4$ **teaspoon cinnamon**
$^1/_8$ **teaspoon nutmeg**
**pinch saffron**
**1–2 tablespoons brown sugar**
**2 tablespoons minced fresh parsley**

ONE OF THE FOLLOWING:
2 large zucchini, sliced; 2 large cucumbers, sliced and peeled; 1 small pumpkin or 1 large butternut squash, skinned, seeded, and cubed

1. Brown the pork with salt in a heavy skillet. Drain off excess fat and put aside.
2. Sauté onions in butter until transparent.
3. Place stock in soup pot and add pork, onions, squash, spices, brown sugar, and parsley. Add salt to taste.
4. Simmer covered about 10 minutes or until squash is soft but firm.

SERVES 6

* John Gerard, *Leaves from Gerard's Herball* (New York, 1969), p. 184.

*Perrey of Peson*  Take peson and seeth hem saft and cover hem til thei berst. Thenne take up hem, and cole hem thurgh a cloth; take oynons, and mynce hem, and seeth hem in the same sewe and oile therewith; cast thereto sugar, salt, and saffron, and seeth hem wel thereafter, and serve hem forth.

*Purée of Peas*  Take peas and boil them until they are soft. Cover them until they burst. Then take them out and strain them through a cloth. Take onions and mince them and boil them in the same stew, adding oil. Cast on sugar, salt, and saffron, and boil them well after that and serve them forth.

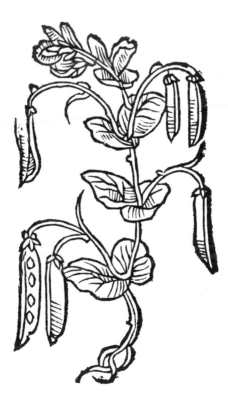

# purée of peas

Here is an exotic sweet pea soup:

    3 cups chicken broth
    3 pounds green peas, shelled
    1 large onion, minced
    2 tablespoons brown sugar
    $^3/_8$ teaspoon salt
    $^3/_8$ teaspoon saffron
    optional garnish: freshly ground pepper

1. Bring chicken broth to a boil.
2. Add remaining ingredients to the broth. Cover and cook over medium flame about 12 to 15 minutes or until peas are soft.
3. Push ingredients through the fine blade of a food mill or purée them in a blender.
4. Return the purée to a pot and simmer to rewarm.
5. Serve in soup bowls. Garnish with a twist of freshly ground pepper if you like.

SERVES 4

Of the shepe . . . of whos hede boylled . . . there cometh a gely and an oynement.

LYDGATE
*Hors, Shepe and Goos* (c. 1470)

*Gele of Fysshe*  Take tenches, pykes, eelys, turbut, and plays. Kerve hem to pecys. Scalde hem and waisshe hem clene. Drye hem with a cloth. Do hem in a pane. Do thereto half vynegar and half wyne and seeth it wel, and take the fysshe and pyke it clene. Cole the broth thurgh a cloth into an erthen pane. Do thereto powder of peper and safron ynowh. Lat it seeth and skym it wel whan it is ysode. Dos the grees clene. Cowche fysshe on chargeors and cole the sewe thorow a cloth onoward, and serve it forth.

*Fish Aspic*  Take tench, pike, eel, turbot, and plaice. Carve them into pieces. Scald them and wash them clean. Dry them with a cloth, and put them into a pan. Add equal parts of vinegar and wine and boil it well. Then take the fish and pick it clean. Strain the broth through a cloth into an earthenware pan. Add ground pepper and a good amount of saffron. Let it boil and skim the top when it is cooked. Remove all of the grease [from the top]. Place the fish on large platters and strain the stock through a cloth onto it, and serve it forth.

# fish aspic

Jellies were often served at great feasts, traditionally at the beginning of the third course. They were made with cow's and pig's feet, as well as with fish bones. There are no indications that the jellies were molded, but it would certainly be in the aesthetic tradition of the medieval feast for you to create a sculptured aspic.

This fish jelly is quite pungent; complement it with lettuce or watercress and some bland raw vegetables such as cauliflower florets or carrot strips.

> 2 $\frac{1}{2}$ pounds of one or a combination of the following: tench, pike, eel, turbot, or plaice, cleaned (include the bones and head of at least one fish to provide the gelatin)
> 1 cup white wine

    1 cup wine vinegar *or* ¹/₂ cup vinegar and
      ¹/₂ cup fish stock if you wish to temper the
      acidity
    ¹/₄ teaspoon saffron
    ¹/₈ teaspoon (or more) freshly ground pepper
    garnish: lettuce or watercress, and raw
      vegetables

1. Place fish (including head) in wine and vinegar and bring to a boil in an earthenware or porcelain pan.
2. Cover and simmer about 15 minutes or until fish begins to flake.
3. Remove fish from liquid. Pick over fish and discard bones and head. Break into chunks and place fish on platter. Set aside.
4. Strain fish broth through a fine-meshed strainer or a cheesecloth.
5. Return broth to pan and add saffron and pepper. Simmer over a gentle flame for about 15 to 20 minutes, skimming the grease off occasionally. Check seasoning.
6. Place fish in a mold. Pour broth over it through strainer.
7. Refrigerate a few hours.
8. Unmold and serve chilled over lettuce or watercress, decorated with vegetables.

SERVES 4–6

47

*Tart de Bry*   Take a crust ynche depe in a trape. Take yolkes of ayren rawe and chese ruayn and medle it and the yolkes together. And do thereto powdor gynger, sugar, safron and salt. Do it in a trape, bake it, and serve it forth.

*Brie Tart*   Take a crust an inch deep in a baking dish. Take raw egg yolks and "ruayn" cheese* and mix it and the yolks together. Add powdered ginger, sugar, saffron and salt. Put it into a baking dish, bake it, and serve it forth.

# bRI€ TART

"Cheese is milk's leap to immortality," Clifton Fadiman once observed.

According to Boorde there were five basic types of cheeses in the Middle Ages:

> Grenc chese is not called grene by the reason of colour, but for the newness of it. . . . Softe chese, not to new nor to olde, is best. . . . Harde chese is hote and dry, and euyll to dygest. Spermyse is a chese the which is made with curdes and with the juce of herbes. . . . Yet besyde these iiii [4] natures of chese, there is a chese called rewene chese, the whiche, yf it be well orderyd, doth passe [surpass] all other cheses.

\* "Ruayn" cheese was a fine-quality fatty cheese made from the milk of cows that had grazed on the autumn grasses of hayfields after the harvest.

Two variations for the Brie tart are offered. The first follows the original recipe closely with delicious results. The second calls for cream and is considerably richer. Both are prepared according to the same instructions.

FIRST VARIATION
8-inch uncooked pie pastry
1 pound young Brie cheese
6 egg yolks, beaten
$1/8$ teaspoon saffron
$3/4$ teaspoon light brown sugar
$3/8$ teaspoon powdered ginger
salt

SECOND VARIATION
8-inch uncooked pie pastry
$1/2$ pound young Brie cheese
$1/2$ cup heavy cream
3 eggs, lightly beaten
$1/8$ $1/4$ teaspoon powdered ginger
$1/8$ teaspoon saffron
$1/2$ teaspoon brown sugar
salt

1. Bake pie pastry at 425° for 10 minutes. Let cool.
2. Remove rind from Brie. Optional: cut rind into pieces about an inch square and sprinkle evenly on pie crust. This will give the tart a stronger cheese flavor.
3. Combine Brie with remaining ingredients in a blender or with an egg beater. Add salt to taste: the amount will depend on the age of the Brie and whether or not you use the rind. Mixture should be smooth.
4. Pour liquid into pastry shell.
5. Bake at 350° for 30 to 40 minutes or until set and brown on top.

FIRST VARIATION SERVES 8–10;
SECOND SERVES 10–12

# ENTRÉES

## We shule flo [flay] the conyng, ant make roste is loyne.

line from a fourteenth-century song

*Connynges in Cyrip*   Take connynges and seeth hem wel in gode broth. Take wyne greke, and do thereto with a porcion of vynegar and floer of canell, hoole clowes, quybibes hoole, and oother gode spices, with raisons, coraunce and gyngyn ypared and ymynced. Take up the conynges and smyte hem on pecys, and cast hem into the siryppe and seeth hem a litel on the fyre and serve it forth.

*Rabbits in Syrup*   Take rabbits and boil them well in good broth. Take Greek wine and add it with a portion of vinegar and ground cinnamon, whole cloves, whole cubebs, and other good spices with raisins, currants, and minced, pared ginger. Take up the rabbits and smite them into pieces, and cast them into the syrup and boil them a little on the fire and serve it forth.

# RABBiTS iN SYRUP

The cony, a variety of mature rabbit, is not mentioned in English literature before the Norman period, and certainly was not native to England. But by the late Middle Ages it was a popular meat, and there are many recipes for cooking it. *Conyng* was served at Henry IV's coronation feast.

This dish, with its sweet, highly spiced syrup, might be served over rice.

> $2\frac{1}{2}$-pound rabbit (or chicken), cut into pieces
> $\frac{1}{3}$ cup flour seasoned with salt and pepper
> 3 tablespoons oil
> 3 cups Muscatel, Vernaccia, or any sweet, heavy wine
> 4 tablespoons cider vinegar
> $\frac{1}{4}$ cup raisins
> $\frac{1}{2}$ cup currants
> $\frac{1}{4}$ teaspoon cinnamon
> 2 teaspoons freshly minced ginger
> 20 cubebs, finely ground
> 10 cloves, finely ground (scant $\frac{1}{4}$ teaspoon)

1. Dredge rabbit in seasoned flour, and brown in oil in a heavy skillet.
2. In the top of a double boiler, combine remaining ingredients. Heat and stir until blended. Check seasoning.
3. Pour syrup over the rabbit, stirring to combine the dregs. Cover and cook over a gentle flame for about 40 minutes or until rabbit is tender.

SERVES 4

Cookes and heore [their] knaves cryen, "hote pies, hote!"

LANGLAND
*Piers Plowman* (1362)

*Tartee* Take pork ysode. Hewe it, and bray it. Do thereto ayren, raisons, sugar, and powdor of gynger, powder-douce, and smale briddes there among and white grece. Take prunes, safron, and salt, and make a crust in a trape and do the fars thereinne, and bake it wel and serve it forth.

*Pork Pie* Take cooked pork. Cut it into pieces and pound it. Add eggs, raisins, sugar, powdered ginger, sweet powder, small birds, and white grease. Take prunes, saffron, and salt, and make a crust in a baking tin. Put the stuffing in it, and bake it well and serve it forth.

# pork pie

Like the four and twenty blackbirds made famous by the nursery rhyme, small birds were often baked in a pie:

> When the pie was opened, the birds began to sing.
> Wasn't that a dainty dish to set before a king?

Legend has it that a false crust was baked on top of an empty pie shell. Just before it was served, live birds were placed under the pastry lid.

Our *smale bridde* will have a different fate: it will be cooked and eaten.

54

10-inch uncooked pie pastry

1 Cornish hen, quail, or squab, cut into about
   8 pieces

$1/2$ cup flour, seasoned with salt and pepper

2 tablespoons oil

1 pound lean ground pork

2 eggs

$1/4$ cup raisins

10 prunes, minced

1 teaspoon light brown sugar

$1/2$ teaspoon powdered ginger

$3/4$ teaspoon salt

$3/8$ teaspoon saffron

$1/2$ teaspoon ground anise

1 teaspoon ground fennel

$1/2$ teaspoon ground cloves

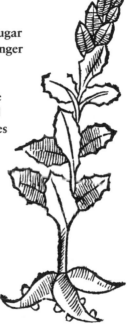

1. Bake pie pastry at 425° for 10 minutes. Let cool.
2. Dredge pieces of fowl in seasoned flour and
   brown in oil until golden.
3. Combine remaining ingredients. Spread about a
   third of the mixture on the pie pastry. Then
   distribute the pieces of fowl evenly on top of it.
   Use the remaining pork mixture to cover the fowl.
4. Bake at 375° for 35 minutes or until pork is
   brown throughout.

SERVES 4–6

"Let furth youre geyse," the fox will preche.
*Towneley Mystery Cycle* (c. 1460)

*Sawse Madame* Take sawge, parsel, ysope and savray, quinces and peers, garlek and grapes, and fylle the gees therewith and sowe the hole that no greece come oute and roost hem wel, and kepe the grece that fallith thereof. Take galyntyne and grece and do in a possynet. Whan the gees buth rosted ynouh, take and smyte hem on pecys, and that, tat is withinne, and do it in a possynet and put thereinne wyne, if it be to thyk. Do thereto powdor of galyngale, powdor-douce and salt, and boyle the sawse and dresse the gees in disshes, and lay the sowe onoward.

*Goose in Sauce Madame* Take sage, parsley, hyssop, savory, quinces, pears, garlic, and grapes, and fill the goose with it. Sew the hole so that no grease can escape, and roast it well. Reserve the drippings. Take galantine and grease and put them in a small pot. When the goose is roasted enough, carve it into pieces and put the stuffing and the pieces into a pot. Add wine if it is too thick. Add powdered galingale, sweet powder, and salt, and boil the sauce. Arrange pieces of the goose on dishes and place the sauce on top.

# GOOSE IN SAUCE MADAME

Since poultry was fed natural grains and allowed to run freely, its taste was distinctly gamy. Perhaps an organically raised or wild goose would come closer in taste to a medieval bird.

Using the high-temperature roasting method explained opposite, allow 15 to 16 minutes per pound for the total weight of goose plus stuffing (about 2 ½ to 3 hours for a 9-pound bird). When goose is cooked, the legs can be moved up and down freely.

9-pound goose

4 tablespoons salt

3 cups each cored and diced pears and quinces
   (if quince is out of season replace with tart
   apples)

2 cups grapes, preferably seedless

15 cloves garlic, peeled

1 teaspoon dried sage

$^1/_2$ cup roughly chopped parsley

2 teaspoons dried hyssop

1 teaspoon dried savory

$^1/_4$ cup galantine (recipe, p. 90)

$^3/_8$ cup red wine

garnish: watercress or parsley

1. Rub goose inside and out with salt.

2. Combine fruits, garlic, sage, parsley, hyssop, and
   savory for stuffing.

3. Stuff goose as full as possible. Sew or skewer
   opening. Place excess stuffing in covered casserole
   and bake separately

4. Put 1 to 2 cups of water in a shallow roasting
   pan. Place goose on its side directly in pan and
   roast at 425° for 1 hour, basting frequently and
   skimming off fat. Keep adding water as it evap-
   orates.

5. Turn goose and roast it on its other side for 30
   minutes; alternate sides every 30 minutes, but for
   final 15 minutes roast goose on its back.

6. When bird is done, remove stuffing.

7. To prepare sauce, combine stuffing, galantine,
   and wine in a large saucepan; stir to blend, and
   heat.

8. Using poultry shears, remove wings and drum-
   sticks and carve goose body into small pieces,
   leaving meat on bone whenever possible.

9. Combine goose pieces with sauce; cover and
   rewarm a few minutes before serving.

10. Serve on a large platter with garnish.

SERVES 8

**The wombe oway he bare; the noubles he yf [gave] to mede [reward].**

*Sir Tristrem* (c. 1320)

*Noumbles*   Take noumbles of deer, other of other beest. Perboile hem. Kerf hem to dyce. Take the self broth or better. Take brede and grynde with the broth and temper it up with a gode qantitie of vynegar and wyne. Take the oynonns and perboyle hem, and mynce hem small and do thereto. Color it with blode, and do thereto powdor-fort and salt, and boyle it well, and serve it forth.

*Innards*   Take the entrails of the deer or of another beast and parboil them. Carve them into dice. Take the same broth or better. Combine ground bread with the broth and mix it with a good quantity of vinegar and wine. Take the onions and parboil them and mince them small and add them. Color it with blood and add strong powder and salt and boil it well and serve it forth.

# INNARÐS

The quote opposite indicates the tradition of feeding entrails to the dogs as a reward after a successful hunt. But *noumbles* were considered suitable fare for the feast and, in fact, were served at one bishop's fifteenth-century repast. In more recent years, however, *noumbles* have not been so highly regarded, as attested by the meaning of our phrase "to eat humble pie" (i.e., "to eat numble pie," said quickly).

*Noumbles* include all of the inner parts of the beast, particularly the digestive organs. Other innards may be substituted or used in combination with the tripe, but do some reading on suggested precooking preparations beforehand.

    2 pounds honeycomb tripe (rinsed thoroughly,
        rubbed with salt, then rinsed again)
    2 quarts boiling water with 2 tablespoons salt
    5 cups vegetable or beef stock
    $^{1}/_{2}$ cup red wine
    1 cup minced onions
    1 teaspoon powdered ginger
    1 tablespoon vinegar (or more, to taste)
    salt to taste
    1 cup bread crumbs (optional)
    garnish: minced fresh parsley

1. Place tripe into boiling salted water. Boil for 15 minutes. Drain, and discard water.
2. Cut tripe into half-inch cubes.
3. Place remaining ingredients (except garnish) in a large soup pot and bring to a boil.
4. Add tripe.
5. Reduce flame and simmer, covered, for $2^{1}/_{2}$ to 3 hours until tripe is tender.
6. Serve in soup bowls and garnish with parsley.

SERVES 6

**A Monk, whan he is reccheless [reckless],**
**Is likned til [to] a fissh that is waterlees.**

CHAUCER
"Prologue" to the *Canterbury Tales* (c. 1386)

*Egurdouce of Fysshe* Take loches, other tenches, other
solys. Smyte hem on pecys. Fry hem in oyle. Take half wyne,
half vynegar and sugar, and make a siryp. Do thereto oynons
icowe, raisons corance and grete raysons. Do thereto hole
spices, gode powdors, and salt. Messe the fysshe and lay the
sewe above, and serve it forth.

*Sweet and Sour Fish* Take loaches, tenches, or soles. Smite
them into pieces. Fry them in oil. Take equal parts of wine and
vinegar with sugar and make a syrup. Add minced onions,
currants, and raisins. Add whole spices, good powders, and
salt. Divide the fish into portions, pour the sauce on top, and
serve it forth.

# SWEET AND SOUR FISH

Loach and tench are both fresh-water fish of the carp family. The sweet and sour sauce provides a tangy contrast to the taste of the fish, and the vinegar cuts into the oiliness. This dish is served to best advantage over rice.

> 2 pounds carp, sole, or any other firm fish fillets
> $^1/_4$ cup flour
> 1 medium onion, minced
> $^3/_4$ cup white wine
> $^3/_4$ cup (or less) cider vinegar
> 4 tablespoons brown sugar
> 12 cubebs, coarsely crushed
> scant $^1/_4$ teaspoon cloves
> pinch mace
> salt to taste
> $^1/_4$ cup each currants and raisins

1. Cut fillets into large chunks and dredge them in flour.
2. Heat oil in a large heavy saucepan and sauté onion until transparent.
3. Add fish chunks and brown them.
4. In a bowl combine remaining ingredients for sauce.
5. Pour liquid over browned fish and onions. Turn off flame. Cover and allow to marinate about 15 minutes.
6. Simmer uncovered about 5 minutes or until fish flakes and liquid is slightly reduced.

SERVES 4

*Tart de Brymlent*  Take fyges and raysons and waisshe hem in wyne, and grinde hem smale with apples and peres clene ypiked. Take hem up and cast hem in a pot with wyne and sugar. Take salwar salmon ysode other codlyng other haddok and bray hem smale and do thereto white powdors and hool spices and salt and seeth it, and whanneit is sode ynowz, take it up, and do it in a vessel, and lat it kele. Make a coffyn an ynche depe and do the fars therein. Plant it bove with prunes and damysyns, take the stones out, and with dates quarte rede, and piked clene, and cover the coffyn and bake it wel and serve it forth.

*Tart for Mid-Lent*  Take figs and raisins and wash them in wine and grind them small with apples and pears picked clean. Take them up and cast them into a pot with wine and sugar. Take boiled calver salmon, codling, or haddock and beat them small. Add white powders, whole spices, and salt, and boil it, and when it is boiled enough, take it up and put it into a vessel and let it cool. Make a pie pastry an inch deep, and put the farce into it. Place prunes and damsons above (take the stones out), and dates quartered and picked clean, and cover the pie, and bake it well, and serve it forth.

# TART FOR MID-LENT

Much fish was eaten in the Middle Ages, since there were a large number of meatless Lenten days. The term "calver salmon" is not understood, but perhaps suggests a pickled or salted fish. I tried the recipe with pickled salmon and did not care for it. But with fresh fish it is unusual and delicious.

If you wish to leave the pastry cover off, arrange most of the fish on the top for visual effect (the salmon pink is striking against the fruit) and bake about 15 minutes less, or until fish flakes.

8-inch uncooked pie pastry, plus pastry lid
2 tablespoons butter
2 pears, peeled, cored, and thinly sliced
2 apples, peeled, cored, and thinly sliced
1 cup good-quality white wine
2 tablespoons lemon juice
2 tablespoons brown sugar
5 cubebs, finely crushed
$\frac{1}{8}$ teaspoon cloves
$\frac{1}{8}$ teaspoon nutmeg
$\frac{1}{4}$ teaspoon cinnamon
$\frac{1}{2}$ cup raisins
10 prunes, minced
6 dates, minced
6 dried figs, minced
$1\frac{1}{2}$ pounds salmon, cod, or haddock (or a mixture), cut into $1\frac{1}{2}$-inch chunks, lightly salted, and sprinkled with 2 tablespoons lemon juice
3 tablespoons damson or red currant jelly
2 tablespoons milk

1. Bake pie pastry bottom at 425° for 10 minutes. Let cool.
2. Melt butter in a large heavy skillet and toss pear and apple slices in it until they are lightly coated.
3. Combine wine, lemon juice, brown sugar, spices, and dried fruits, and add to mixture in skillet. Cover and simmer about 15 minutes or until fresh fruit is soft but still firm.
4. Check seasoning, and drain off excess liquid.
5. Paint jelly on pie crust.
6. Combine fish chunks with fruits and place mixture into crust.
7. Cover pie with pastry lid, flute edges, and paint lid with milk.
8. Bake at 375° for 30 to 40 minutes or until crust is golden.

SERVES 6–8

I is ful wight [as clever a creature], god waat [knows],
as is a raa [roe].

CHAUCER
"Reeve's Tale" (c. 1386)

*Roo Broth*  Take the lire of the deer other of the roo; parboile
it on smale peces. Seeth it wel, half in water, and half in wyne.
Take brede, and bray it with the self broth, and drawe blode
thereto, and lat it seeth togedre with powdor-fort of gynger,
other of cannell and macys, with a grete porcionn of vynegar,
with raysons of corannte.

*Venison Stew*  Take the flesh of the deer or the roe. Parboil it
in small pieces. Cook it well in equal parts of water and wine.
Take bread and crush it in the broth. Add blood and let it cook
together with strong powder of ginger or of cinnamon and
mace. Add a great portion of vinegar and some currants.

# VENISON STEW

The hunt for game was a highly ritualized activity in
the Middle Ages. In the romance *Tristan*, there is a
long section describing the hero's masterful talent in
carving a freshly slain deer. Tristan's true nobility is
revealed by his knowledge of this special, almost
sacred art.

Parboiling is frequently the first step in a medieval
recipe. Fresh meat had to be tenderized, and salted
meat softened. Since most of our meat has been aged,
this step can be eliminated.

There is much "broth" in this stew, so you may
wish to serve it over noodles or rice in deep bowls.

3 tablespoons bacon fat
1 medium onion, minced
2 pounds venison, cut into $1\frac{1}{2}$-inch cubes
    (beef or veal stewing meat may be substituted)
$\frac{1}{4}$ cup flour
$1\frac{1}{2}$ cups boiling water or beef stock
$1\frac{1}{2}$ cups red wine

2 teaspoons finely minced fresh ginger, *or*
    1 teaspoon powdered ginger
1 tablespoon (or more) vinegar
$^1/_2$ cup currants
salt
$^1/_2$ cup bread crumbs (optional)
fresh deer blood, to taste, if available

1. Melt bacon fat in a large saucepan.
2. Sauté onion in fat until it is transparent.
3. Dredge venison cubes in flour.
4. Brown cubes in skillet, combining them with onions.
5. Combine water or stock, wine, ginger, vinegar, currants, and salt to taste. Stir to blend.
6. Pour liquid over meat.
7. Cover and simmer about 2 $^1/_2$ hours or until meat is tender.
8. Add bread crumbs to thicken if desired.
9. If blood is available, remove pot from flame a few moments before adding it, as it should not boil. The blood will thicken and flavor the sauce as well as darken the color.

SERVES 4 6

**The capon is a cocke made as it were female by kervynge away of his gendringe stones.**

BARTHOLOMAEUS ANGLICUS
*De proprietatibus rerum*
(translated into Middle English by Trevisa, 1398)

*Douce Ame*  Take gode cowe mylke and do it in a pot. Take parsel, sawge, ysope, savray and oother gode herbes. Hewe hem, and do hem in the mylke and seeth hem. Take capons half yrosted and smyte hem on pecys and do thereto pynes and hony clarified. Salt it and color it with safron and serve it forth.

*Sweet Measure: Capon in Milk and Honey*  Take good cow's milk and put it into a pot. Take parsley, sage, hyssop, savory, and other good herbs. Chop them, put them in the milk, and cook them. Take half-roasted capons and hack them into pieces. Also add pine nuts and clarified honey. Salt it and color it with saffron, and serve it forth.

# SWEET MEASURE:
# CAPON IN MILK AND HONEY

This golden dish is resplendent and served to best advantage over plain white rice. Different types of honey will produce interesting variations in flavor.

> 3–4-pound capon (or chicken), cut into
>     serving pieces
> $\frac{1}{2}$ cup flour mixed with $\frac{1}{2}$ teaspoon salt and
>     $\frac{1}{8}$ teaspoon freshly ground pepper
> 3 tablespoons oil
> 3 cups milk
> $\frac{1}{3}$ cup honey
> 3 tablespoons minced fresh parsley
> 2 small leaves fresh sage, minced, *or*
>     $\frac{1}{4}$ teaspoon dried
> 1 teaspoon hyssop
> $\frac{1}{2}$ teaspoon savory
> $\frac{1}{4}$–$\frac{1}{2}$ teaspoon saffron
> $\frac{1}{2}$ teaspoon salt
> $\frac{1}{8}$ teaspoon freshly ground pepper
> $\frac{1}{3}$ cup pine nuts

1. Dredge fowl in flour mixture.
2. Brown the pieces in oil in a large heavy saucepan until golden on both sides.
3. Combine milk, honey, herbs, salt, and pepper in a bowl.
4. Pour liquid over browned fowl in saucepan, stirring to combine drippings with the sauce.
5. Cover and simmer about 20 minutes or until fowl is tender.
6. Check seasoning.
7. Stir in pine nuts just before serving.

SERVES 4–6

A Cook they hadde with hem for the nones
To boille the chiknes with the marybones.

CHAUCER
"Prologue" to the *Canterbury Tales* (c. 1386)

*Chykens in Hocchee*  Take chykenns and scald hem. Take
parsel and sawge without eny other erbes. Take garlec and
grapes and stoppe the chikens ful, and seeth hem in good broth
so that they may esely be boyled thereinee. Messe hem and
cast thereto powdor douce.

*Chickens in Hotchpot*  Take chickens and scald them. Take
parsley and sage without any other herbs. Take garlic and
grapes and stuff the chickens full and cook them in good broth
so that they may easily be boiled within. Divide them into
portions and cast sweet powder on top.

# chickens in hotchpot

The culinary term "hotchpot" (the ancestor of our
word "hodgepodge") refers to a combination of di-
verse ingredients such as this stuffed chicken in soup.

Although menus indicate that fowl was most often
roasted for the feast, recipes from the *Forme of Cury*
indicate that they were frequently boiled, stuffed or
unstuffed, for daily use. You may wish to experiment
by substituting pheasant, partridge, capon, or any
game bird for chicken in the above recipe. You can
vary the broth by flavoring it to taste with whole (or
coarsely ground) peppercorns, cinnamon, or such
sweet aromatic spices as aniseed, fennel seed, and
nutmeg.

Or, you might stuff the bird as directed and roast it.

> 4–5-pound stewing chicken, including feet,
>    neck, and giblets
> 6 cups water
> 1 teaspoon salt
> 8 tablespoons minced fresh parsley

$^{1}/_{2}$ teaspoon dried sage
12 cloves garlic, peeled
$^{3}/_{4}$ pound grapes, preferably seedless
**garnish: nutmeg or crushed anise or fennel seeds**

1. Place chicken in colander and scald with boiling water. Remove fat from cavity opening.
2. Bring water and salt to a boil.
3. Stuff bird with 6 tablespoons of the parsley and the sage, garlic, and grapes.
4. Place chicken in boiling water. Return to a boil; cover and lower heat.
5. Allow to simmer about an hour or until chicken is tender. About 15 minutes before it is finished, add the remaining parsley to the broth.
6. Cut chicken into portions, and serve together with stuffing and liquid in soup bowls.
7. Sprinkle each serving with your choice of nutmeg, crushed anise, or fennel seeds.

SERVES 6–8

69

**For blancmange, that made he with the best.**

CHAUCER
"Prologue" to the *Canterbury Tales* (c. 1386)

*Blank-Mang* Take capons and seeth hem. Thenne take hem up. Take almandes blanced. Grynd hem and alay hem up with the same broth. Cast the mylk in a pot. Waisshe rys and do thereto and lat it seeth. Thanne take brawn of caponns. Teere it small and do thereto. Take white greece, sugar, and salt, and cast thereinne. Lat it seeth. Then mess it forth and florish it with ancys in confyt rede other whyte and with almandes fryed in oyle and serve it forth.

*White-Dish* Take capons and cook them. Then remove them from the pot. Take blanched almonds. Grind them and mix them with the capon broth. Cast the [almond] milk in a pot. Wash rice and add it and let it cook. Then take flesh of capons, tear it small, and add it. Take white grease, sugar, and salt, and cast them in. Let it cook. Then divide it into portions and garnish it with red or white confectioned anise and with almonds fried in oil, and serve it forth.

70

# white-dish

It is no surprise that Chaucer's Cook knew how to make *blank-mang*, for it was one of the most popular dishes of the Middle Ages both in England and on the Continent. Its flavor is as delicate as its appearance.

2 large capon or chicken breasts
2 1/2 cups water
1 1/4 teaspoons salt
1/2 cup blanched almonds
2 tablespoons ice water
1 cup rice
1 tablespoon butter
4 teaspoons light brown sugar
garnishes:
   3–4 tablespoons crushed aniseed
   1/4 cup slivered blanched almonds fried in
     2 tablespoons oil
   sprigs of watercress or parsley

1. Boil breasts gently in the 2 1/2 cups water and 1/4 teaspoon salt in a covered pan 10 to 15 minutes or until done.
2. Remove fowl and set aside, reserving broth.
3. Grind almonds with ice water in a blender or with mortar and pestle.
4. Combine 2 cups of broth with almonds to make almond milk. Let stand about 10 minutes, stirring occasionally.
5. Cook rice in almond milk with 1 teaspoon salt, butter, and brown sugar until almost done.
6. Meanwhile, bone and dice fowl.
7. Just before rice is done, add fowl; stir to distribute evenly, and finish cooking.
8. Before serving, garnish with aniseed and almonds. Decorate with sprigs of watercress or parsley.

SERVES 4–6

# side dishes

**Wel loved he garleek, oynons, and eek [also] lekes.**

CHAUCER
"Prologue" to the *Canterbury Tales* (c. 1386)

*Aquapatys*   Pill garlec and cast it in a pot with water and oile and seeth it. Do thereto safron, salt, and powdor-fort and dresse it forth hool.

*Boiled Garlic*   Peel garlic. Cast it into a pot with water and oil, and boil it. Add saffron, salt, and strong powder. Serve it forth whole.

# boileb garlic

In the Middle Ages, garlic was considered a vegetable and a medicinal herb. Boorde claims: "Garlyke, of all rootes is used and most praysed in Lombardy, and other countres anexed to it; for it doth open the breste, and it doth kyll all maner of wormes in a mans bely."

When prepared in the following manner, garlic has a surprisingly delicate flavor and a texture somewhat like baked potato. But here is a thirteenth-century remedy to reassure those disbelievers among you: "The strong smell of garlic is removed by eating boiled beans or lentils, or by chewing zedoary or garden mint of the wild sort, and drinking a little vinegar afterwards."*

After tasting this dish, you will wonder how such a subtle vegetable got imprisoned in the category of a seasoning.

> 1 cup water
> cloves of 6 bulbs of garlic, peeled
> 3 tablespoons butter or oil
> $^1/_8$ teaspoon saffron
> $^1/_8$ teaspoon salt
> $^1/_4$ teaspoon cinnamon
> pinch mace
> garnish: 1 tablespoon minced fresh parsley

1. Bring water to a boil.
2. Add garlic cloves, butter or oil, saffron, salt, cinnamon, and mace.
3. Cover and cook over medium flame about 7 minutes or until garlic is easily pierced with a fork.
4. Drain and serve with a garnish of parsley.

SERVES 4–6

* Way, p. 25.

[Old men] have an hoor [hoary] head and a grene tayl,
as hath a leek.

CHAUCER
"Reeve's Prologue" (c. 1386)

*Funges*   Take funges, and pare hem clene and dyce hem. Take
leke, and shred hym small and do hym to seeth in gode broth.
Color it with safron, and do there-inne powder-fort.

*Mushrooms (and Leeks)*   Take mushrooms and pare them
clean and dice them. Take leek and shred it small and cook
it in good broth. Color it with saffron and add strong spices.

# mushrooms and leeks

It is difficult to know what particular varieties of
mushrooms were eaten in medieval England. One
Latin treatise of the thirteenth century mentions that
eating truffles generates colic, but that other *fungi* are
actually much worse: some species so constrict the
throat as to prove fatal.*

King Richard's cooks apparently knew a variety of
edible mushrooms and suggest preparing them with
leeks. This is a culinary marriage made in heaven.

> 8 small leeks
> 3 tablespoons butter
> 1 $^1/_2$ pounds large mushrooms, quartered
> 1 cup vegetable or chicken stock
> $^1/_2$ teaspoon brown sugar
> $^1/_8$ teaspoon saffron
> $^1/_2$ teaspoon minced fresh ginger
> beurre manié: 3 tablespoons soft butter com-
>     bined with 3 tablespoons white flour
> salt and freshly ground pepper

* Way, p. 30.

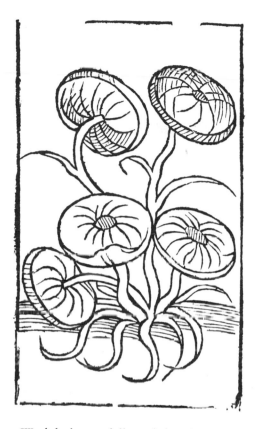

1. Wash leeks carefully and slice them into rings, discarding roots and green tops.
2. Sauté leeks in butter in a large heavy skillet until they begin to wilt. Then add mushrooms and toss to coat.
3. Combine stock, sugar, saffron, and ginger, and pour the liquid over vegetables.
4. Simmer covered for about 2 minutes.
5. Add beurre manié, stirring rapidly over a low flame until liquid thickens and vegetables are evenly glazed.
6. Add salt and pepper to taste.

SERVES 4–6

He toke an erbe, and robbed [rubbed] Charlemagnes noose and his lippes wyth it.

CAXTON
*Sonnes of Aymon* (c. 1489)

*Erbolate*  Take parsel, myntes, saverey, and sauge, tansey, vervayn, clarry, rewe, ditayn, fenel, southrenwode. Hewe hem and grinde hem smale. Medle hem up with ayren. Do butter in a trape and do the fars thereto, and bake, and messe forth.

*Baked Herbed Eggs*  Take parsley, mint, savory, sage, tansy, vervain, clary, rue, dittany, fennel, southernwood. Chop them and grind them small. Mix them with eggs. Put butter in a baking dish and put the mixture in it. Bake it and serve it in portions.

# BAKED HERBED EGGS

This recipe is one which exemplifies Boorde's belief that "a good cook is half a physician." All of the herbs included were thought to have beneficial medicinal value.

We think of eating an herb omelet for breakfast, but the medieval nobleman preferred to start the day with "sops" in wine. Most likely, *erbolate* would have been eaten by someone concerned about his digestion— perhaps as a light snack before retiring.

The herbs would have been taken fresh from the castle garden. Although one might expect some of the herbs like rue and tansy to be blanched before use to draw out some of the bitter juices, it seems from the recipe that they were taken "straight." If you are lucky enough to have fresh herbs, mince approximately twice the amount indicated, eliminate steps 1 and 2, and combine the herbs with the egg mixture.

$^1/_3$ cup hot milk

3 tablespoons dried herbs as available (choose
   from list in translated recipe opposite)

5 eggs, lightly beaten

$^1/_8$ teaspoon salt

2 tablespoons butter

1. Pour milk over dried herbs and stir until they
   have all been coated. Allow the mixture to sit for
   30 minutes, or until the milk is strongly flavored.
2. Strain liquid through a fine mesh strainer.
   Discard herbs.
3. Combine eggs, milk, and salt, beating a few
   moments with a wire whisk.
4. Melt butter in an 8-inch ovenproof skillet or
   baking dish.
5. Pour in egg mixture.
6. Bake in a preheated 325° oven for 35 minutes or
   until eggs are set and top is golden brown.
7. Serve as you would a pie.

SERVES 3–4

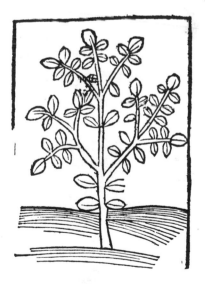

**Beware of saladis, grene metis, and of frutes rawe.**

> JOHN RUSSELL
> *Boke of Nurture* (c. 1460)

*Salat*  Take parsel, sawge, garlec, chibollas, oynons, leek, borage, myntes, porrectes, fenel, and ton tressis, rew, rosemarye, purslayne, lave, and waisshe hem clene. Pike hem, pluk hem small with thyn hond and myng hem wel with rawe oile. Lay on vynegar and salt and serve it forth.

*Salad*  Take parsley, sage, garlic, chibol, onions, leek, borage, mints, porret, fennel, and watercress, rue, rosemary, purslane, laver, and wash them clean. Pick them over, pluck them into small pieces with your hand, and mix them well with raw oil. Add vinegar and salt and serve it forth.

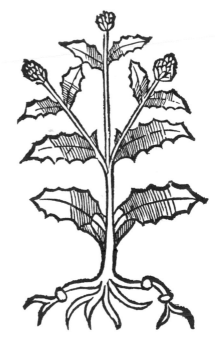

## SALAꝺ

Here is an interesting and unusual salad which you can prepare with whatever combination of ingredients is available. Shred the greens and mince the garlic, leeks, and onions very finely. Despite John Russell's admonition (see quotation) to beware of eating the raw greens, the inclusion of this recipe in the *Forme of Cury* is a testimony to the practice of eating them.

Various types of oil were available in the Middle Ages in England. In John Trevisa's translation of Bartholomew the Englishman's thirteenth-century treatise on "The Nature of Things," we read: "Many divers oile is pressedde out of many divers thinges and some oile is semple: as oile of olife, oile of nottes, oile of popie . . . and some oile is medled and compowned." Since the oils were "raw," or unrefined, they would have retained the distinctive flavor of their sources, much the way olive oil does today.

The most common vinegar was undoubtedly wine-based, since wines quickly turned acidic due to improper sealing of casks. However, pear vinegar was also used, as we can see from the following Middle English translation of the Latin treatise on *Husbandry* by Palladius. *Aysell* (eisell) is an obsolete word for vinegar.

> Of peres soure and wilde it is noo wronge
> Aysell to bringe, all ripe yf that thai be
> Ytake and kepte upheped daies three.
>
> Then in a vessel se that thai be doo
> And water with of rayne or of the welle,
> Then hele it faire, or se that it be soo,
> And daies therin lette hem dwelle.
> Now aisel take unto thine use, or selle.
> But se what quantitee therof thou take
> With water up the summe ayenie thou make.

Take wild and sour pears and let them ripen in heaps for three days. Put them into a vessel with rain or well water, cover it, and let them sit for many days. Then use the eisell yourself or sell it, and if you wish to make a larger quantity, add a little water.

For the dressing, you may use the combination of three parts oil to one part vinegar. Since the herbs are part of the salad, only salt to taste is recommended as a seasoning.

Ffesauntez enflureschit in flammande [flaming] silver with darielles [pastries] endordide, and daynteez ynewe [enough].

*Morte Arthure* (1400)

*For to Make Pomes Dorryle and Other Things*   Take the lire of pork rawe and grynde it smale. Medle it up with powdor-fort, safron, and salt and do raisons of corance. Make balles thereof and wete it wele in white of ayren and do it to seeth in boillyng water. Take hem up and put hem on a spyt. Rost hem wel and take parsel ygronde and wryng it up with ayren and a plenty of floer and lat erne aboyte the spyt. And if thou wilt, take for parsel, safron, and serve it forth.

*To Make Golden Apples and Other Things*   Take the flesh of raw pork and grind it small. Mix it up with strong powder, saffron, salt, and currants. Roll it into balls and wet it well in egg white and cook it in boiling water. Take them out and put them on a spit. Roast them well. Take ground parsley and press it together with eggs and plenty of flour and let the paste flow from above the spit. And if you wish, take saffron instead of parsley and serve it forth.

# TO MAKE GOLDEN APPLES AND OTHER THINGS

What follows is a lesson in the popular art of endoring food and turning ground pork into golden apples. This same endoring paste may be painted on any fowl before roasting it. (You may wish to do some "touching up" at the halfway point.) For green instead of golden apples, substitute finely minced parsley for saffron.

Another manuscript recipe for *pomes dorryle* calls for honey, and this makes a delicious addition. Drip it on top of the pork balls just before serving. Arrange them on a platter set off with fried apple slices.

$^3/_4$ pound ground pork
$^1/_4$ pound spicy pork sausage removed from
   casing
$^1/_2$ teaspoon salt
$^1/_2$ teaspoon nutmeg
$^1/_2$ teaspoon ground cloves
5 crushed cubebs   ½ All spice/ half pepper
1 egg
$^1/_2$ cup currants
3 egg yolks
$^1/_8$ teaspoon saffron
1–2 tablespoons flour
2–3 tablespoons honey
garnish: thin slices of apple fried in 2 tablespoons butter and sprinkled lightly with
   cinnamon

1. In a large bowl, combine pork, sausage, salt,
   nutmeg, cloves, cubebs, egg, and currants.
2. Shape into 10 to 12 meat balls about 1$^1/_4$ inches
   in diameter.
3. Bake on a rack in a pan at 350° for 20 minutes.
4. Cool, then refrigerate at least 30 minutes.
5. Meanwhile, prepare endoring paste by blending
   egg yolks, saffron, and flour. The paste should be
   thick, but not dry.
6. Dip pork balls into paste or paint it on with a
   pastry brush.
7. Bake at 350° about 15 minutes or until warm
   throughout. Drip on honey. Serve hot, garnished
   with fried apples.

SERVES 3–4

**Appulle fruture is good hoot, but the cold ye not towche.**

> JOHN RUSSELL
> *Boke of Nurture* (c. 1460)

*Fritors of Pasternakes of Apples*   Take skyrwates and pasternakes and apples and parboile hem. Make a bator of floer and ayren. Cast thereto ale, safron, and salt. Wete hem in the bator, and frye hem in oile or in grece. Do thereto almandes mylk and serve it forth.

*Fritters of Parsnips or of Apples*   Take skirrets, parsnips, and apples, and parboil them. Make a batter of flour and eggs. Cast ale, saffron, and salt into it. Wet them in the batter and fry them in oil or in grease. Pour on almond milk and serve it forth.

# FRiTTERS OF pARSNips
# OR OF Apples

BATTER

Here is a light and tasty batter for any type of fried food. The foamy ale barm acted as a yeast substitute in many medieval recipes. If you add the saffron, let the batter sit about 15 minutes so the color will come out.

84

2 cups white flour
$^1/_2$ teaspoon salt
$^1/_2$ teaspoon saffron (optional)
1 egg
1 $^1/_2$ cups ale at room temperature

Combine all ingredients in a large bowl, stirring until mixture is almost smooth. The batter should be somewhat thick and a bit lumpy.

> YIELD: enough batter for either parsnip
> or apple fritters

## PARSNIP FRITTERS

Unfortunately, parsnips have been relegated to the soup pot or ignored altogether. This recipe allows their delicate, sweet flavor to come through. I've been unable to locate skirrets, but if you can buy or grow them, prepare them as you would the parsnips.

10–12 medium parsnips
6 tablespoons vegetable oil
salt to taste
1 cup broth-based almond milk (optional: see
    p. 116)

1. Scrape parsnips.
2. Cut parsnips in half or thirds lengthwise. Then slice strips from each section.
3. Steam strips in half an inch of boiling water for about 10 minutes, or until they are easily pierced with the tip of a knife.
4. Drain and pat pieces dry.
5. Dip strips into batter.
6. Fry in hot oil until golden on both sides. Drain on paper towels.
7. Sprinkle lightly with salt and arrange on a platter, or pour almond milk over fritters and serve in a bowl.

SERVES 6–8

6 large firm apples (or pears)
6 tablespoons vegetable oil
$^1/_2$ cup confectioner's sugar blended with
   1 teaspoon cinnamon, *or* 1 cup wine- or
   water-based almond milk (see p. 116)

1. Cut apples into slices $^1/_4$ inch thick, starting on
the side and poking out seeds in the central slices.
Don't bother to remove core.
2. Dip slices into batter.
3. Fry in hot oil until both sides are golden brown.
Drain on paper towels.
4. Sprinkle sugar mixture over fritters through a
sieve and arrange on a platter, or serve with
almond milk in a bowl.

SERVES 6–8

## Von Apffelbaumen.

# SAUCES

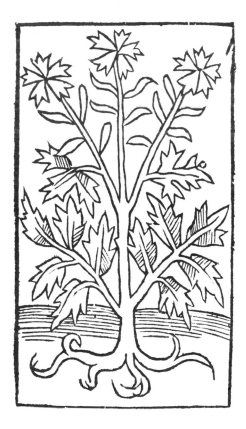

*Sawse Noyre for Capons Yrosted*  Take the lyver of capons
and roost it wele. Take anyse and greynes de Paris, gynger,
canel and a lytill crust of brede. Grinde it smale and grynde it
up with verjous, and with grece of capons.

*Black Sauce for Roasted Capons*  Take the liver of capons
and roast it well. Take anise and grains of paradise, ginger,
cinnamon, and a little crust of bread. Grind it small and combine it with verjuice and with the grease of capons.

# bLACK SAUCE
# FOR ROASTED CApONS

This sauce is full of interesting taste surprises, and
would complement fowl of any kind.

> 2 tablespoons chicken fat
> $^1/_2$ pound capon or chicken livers, minced
> 1 cup verjuice (see glossary; a makeshift
>   verjuice can be prepared by combining
>   $^3/_4$ cup grape juice and $^1/_4$ cup red wine
>   vinegar)
> $^3/_8$ teaspoon each finely ground grains of
>   paradise, aniseed, and powdered ginger
> salt to taste
> $^1/_4$ cup ground bread crusts

1. Melt chicken fat in a medium-sized skillet.
2. Brown livers until there are no more pink spots.
3. Combine verjuice, spices, and salt.
4. Pour over livers and stir to combine dregs with
   liquid.
5. Add bread crumbs and simmer uncovered about
   5 minutes.
6. Check seasoning before serving.

YIELD: 1 $^1/_2$ cups

89

Nas never pyk walwed in galauntyne
As I in love am walwed and ywounde,
For which ful ofte I of myself devyne
That I am trewe Tristam the secounde.

CHAUCER
"To Rosemounde" (c. 1384)

*Galyntyne* Take crustes of brede, and grynde hem smale. Do thereto powdor of galyngale, of canel, gyngynes and salt it. Tempre it with vyngar, and drawe it up thurgh a straynor and mess it forth.

*Galantine* Take bread crusts and grind them small. Add galingale powder, ground cinnamon, ginger, and salt. Mix it with vinegar and pass it through a strainer and serve it forth.

# GALANTINE

The word "galantine" is related etymologically to *gallant*, meaning spirited, dashing, and agreeable. Galantine was served over fillets of pork at the coronation feast of Henry IV, and the recipes often recommend its use over meat, fish, and fowl. Galantine provides the base for a more elaborate concoction in the recipe for *Sawse Madame* (see p. 56).

> 1/3 cup ground bread crusts
> 1 teaspoon powdered galingale
> 1/4 teaspoon cinnamon
> 1/4 teaspoon powdered ginger
> 1 cup beef, chicken, or fish stock
> 2 tablespoons (or more) wine vinegar
> salt to taste

1. Blend crusts with galingale, cinnamon, and ginger.
2. Add remaining ingredients and simmer over gentle flame about 5 minutes, or until desired thickness.
3. Check seasoning before serving.

YIELD: 1 1/2 cups

**This is sawce fyne,
That men calles camelyne.**
*Liber Core Cocorum* (c. 1420)

*Sawse Camelyne* Take raysons of corance and kyrnels of notys and crustes of brede, powdor of gynger, clowes, floer of canel. By it wel togyder and do it thereto. Salt it, temper it up with vynegar and serve it forth.

*Cameline Sauce* Take currants and nuts and crusts of bread, powdered ginger, cloves, cinnamon, and mix them together well. Add salt and vinegar and serve it forth.

# CAMELINE SAUCE

It is thought that this sauce was named for one of its original ingredients, the herb cameline, which is not mentioned in the recipe and is no longer commonly available. If you don't temper the sauce with broth, it is quite pungent, although this quality is set off considerably by the spices and sweet raisins. Try *sawse camelyne* with pork or lamb.

$^3/_4$ cup beef broth
$1^1/_2$ tablespoons (or more) vinegar
$^1/_4$ cup finely crumbled bread crusts
$^1/_{16}$ teaspoon powdered ginger
$^1/_8$ teaspoon powdered cloves
$^1/_4$ teaspoon cinnamon
salt to taste
$^1/_3$ cup raisins
$^1/_3$ cup walnuts

1. Combine all ingredients in a heavy saucepan.
2. Simmer over low heat, stirring to blend, about 5 minutes until raisins are plump and soft.
3. Check seasoning before serving.

YIELD: 1 cup

*Sawse Sarzyne*  Take heppes and make hem clene. Take almandes blanched. Frye hem in oile and braye hem in a mortar with heppes. Drawe it up with rede wyne and do thereinne sugar ynowhg with powdor-fort. Lat it be stondyng and alay it with floer of rys and color it with alkenet and messe it forth and florish it with pomegarnet. If thou wilt, in flesshe day, seeth capons and take the brawn and tese hem smal and do thereto and make the lico of this broth.

*Saracen Sauce*  Take rose hips and clean them. Take blanched almonds. Fry them in oil and pound them in a mortar with the rose hips. Steep them in red wine and add sugar and strong powder. So that it will be thick, mix it with rice flour. Color it with alkanet and serve it forth and sprinkle it with pomegranate seeds. If you wish, on a meat day, cook capons and shred the flesh into small pieces. And for the liquid use this broth.

# SARACEN SAUCE

Saracen soups, stews, and sauces were characterized by the use of almonds as a prime ingredient and pomegranate seeds as a garnish. This Saracen sauce would be tasty with beef.

> $1^1/_2$ teaspoons dried seedless rose hips *or* 3 teaspoons fresh (boiled until tender, seeds removed)
> $^1/_2$ cup red wine
> 2 tablespoons butter
> $^1/_2$ cup blanched almonds
> 2 tablespoons cold water
> $^1/_2$ cup warm red wine
> $^1/_4$ teaspoon cinnamon
> pinch mace
> $^1/_2$ teaspoon sugar
> 1 teaspoon rice flour (optional)
> garnish: pomegranate seeds

1. Crush dried rose hips in a mortar and pestle.
2. Soak them in the $^1/_2$ cup of red wine in a covered jar overnight.
3. Melt butter in a heavy skillet and fry the almonds until they are golden on both sides.
4. Grind almonds in blender with cold water (which prevents them from turning to paste).
5. Soak ground almonds in the warm red wine to make almond milk.
6. Combine almond milk with wine and rose hips mixture in top of a double boiler.
7. Add cinnamon, mace, and sugar, and blend.
8. Warm over gentle steam.
9. The almonds will act as a thickening agent, but if you wish additional thickness, stir in rice flour and cook a few more moments.
10. Check seasoning.
11. Garnish with pomegranate seeds.

YIELD: about 1 cup

*Pevorat for Veel and Venyson*   Take brede and fry it in grece. Draw it up with broth and vynegar. Take thereto powdor of peper and salt and sette it on the fyre. Boile it and messe it forth.

*Pepper Sauce for Veal and Venison*   Take bread and fry it in grease. Steep it in broth and vinegar. Add ground pepper and salt and set it on the fire. Boil it and serve it forth.

# pepper sauce
# for veal and venison

This sauce, now known as *poivrade*, shows off pepper at its finest. For subtle variations in flavor, you might wish to experiment with different types of pepper. *Pevorat* is traditionally served with veal.

> 2 tablespoons butter
> $1/_2$ cup or 1–2 slices bread torn into small pieces
> 1 cup beef or chicken stock
> 1 tablespoon (or more) vinegar
> 10–12 peppercorns, coarsely crushed
> dash salt

1. Melt butter in a heavy skillet and fry bread until it turns golden.
2. In a saucepan, bring stock and vinegar to a boil. Add bread, pepper, and salt, stirring until blended.
3. Simmer over a low flame about 5 minutes.

YIELD: about 1 cup

# DESSERTS

**Appeles and peres that semen very gode,
Ful ofte tyme are roten by the core.**

LYDGATE
*Minor Poems* (1430)

*Leshes Fryed in Lenton*   Drawe a thick almande mylke with
water. Take dates and pyke hem clene, with apples and peeres
and mynce hem with prunes damsyns. Take out the stones out
of the prunes, and kerve the prunes a two. Do thereto raisons,
sugar, floer of canel, hoole macys and clowes, gode powdors
and salt. Color hem up with sandres. Meng thise with oile.
Make a coffyn as thou didest before, and do this fars thereinne,
and bake it wel and serve it forth.

*Fruit Slices Fried for Lent*   Make a thick almond milk with
water. Take dates and pick them over. Take apples and pears
and mince them with damson prunes. Take the stones out of
the prunes and carve the prunes in two. Add raisins, sugar,
cinnamon powder, whole mace and cloves, good spices, and
salt. Color them with sandalwood. Mix these with oil. Make a
coffin as you have done before, and put the stuffing inside, and
bake it well and serve it forth.

96

# FRUIT SLICES
# FRIED FOR LENT

This deep-dish fruit pie is suitable for Lenten days, as
it contains no meat. The almond milk, whose delicate
flavor is hidden by the spices, was probably used as a
thickening agent. Sandalwood tinges the fruit reddish
brown, but in this case does not alter the taste sig-
nificantly.

> 10-inch uncooked pie pastry
> 3 tablespoons butter
> $2\frac{1}{2}$ cups peeled, cored, and thinly sliced apples
> $2\frac{1}{2}$ cups peeled, cored, and thinly sliced pears
> 1 cup mixed dried fruit: raisins, pitted prunes,
>   and halved dates
> $\frac{1}{2}$ cup almond milk (see recipe, p. 116)
> $\frac{1}{2}$ teaspoon red sandalwood powder
> $\frac{1}{4}$ teaspoon cinnamon
> $\frac{1}{4}$ teaspoon powdered cloves
> $\frac{1}{4}$ teaspoon mace
> $\frac{1}{2}$ teaspoon crushed aniseed
> pinch nutmeg
> $\frac{1}{8}$ teaspoon salt

1. Bake pie pastry at 425° for 10 minutes.
2. Melt butter in a heavy skillet.
3. Toss apple and pear slices in butter, and fry
   about 5 minutes.
4. Stir in the dried fruit.
5. Blend almond milk with sandalwood, then stir it
   into the fruit mixture along with remaining
   ingredients.
6. Place mixture in pie pastry.
7. Bake pie at 350° about 35 minutes or until fruit
   is soft.

SERVES 8

# Von Feigen

*Rapé*  Take half fyges and half raison. Pike hem, and waisshe hem in water. Skalde hem in wyne. Bray hem in a mortar, and drawe hem thurgh a straynor. Cast hem in a pot, and therewith powdor of peper, and oother good powdors. Alay it up with floer of rys and color it with sandres. Salt it, and messe it forth.

*Fig and Raisin Purée*  Take equal parts of figs and raisins and pick them over. Wash them in water and scald them in wine. Pound them in a mortar and push them through the strainer. Cast them into a pot and add ground pepper and other good spices. Mix it with rice flour and color it with sandalwood. Add salt and divide it into portions.

# Fig and Raisin Purée

Figs, according to one medieval authority, bring the blood to the surface of the skin and are therefore very good for the complexion.

Here is a rich compote put to advantage with whipped cream and a dash of nutmeg. But you may wish to remain close to the original recipe by garnishing with salt.

Try rapé as a sweet spread on bread or as an accompaniment to lamb or ham.

> 1 1/2 cups minced dried figs
> 1 1/2 cups raisins
> 1 1/2 cups red wine
> 1/2 teaspoon finely minced fresh ginger
> 1/8 teaspoon dried or fresh orange peel
> dash salt and pepper
> 1/2 teaspoon red sandalwood powder dissolved
>    in 2 tablespoons water (optional)

1. Simmer all ingredients in covered pot until fruits become soft.
2. Purée mixture in a blender.
3. Serve warm or chilled.

SERVES 4

**Sche was fayr as is the Rose in May.**

CHAUCER
*The Legend of Good Women* (c. 1385)

*Rosee*   Take thyk mylke as to fore welled. Cast thereto sugar,
a gode porcion pynes, dates ymynced, canel, and powdor
gynger and seeth it and alye it with floers of white rosis and
floer of rys. Cole it, salt it, and messe it forth. If thou wilt, in
stede of almannde mylke, take swete cremes of kyne.

*A Dish Flavored with Rose Petals*   Take the thick milk that
was steeped before [almond milk was prepared in the previous
recipe]. Cast sugar into it and a good portion of pine nuts,
minced dates, cinnamon, and powdered ginger, and cook it
and combine it with flowers of white roses and rice flour. Cool
it, salt it, and divide it into portions to serve. If you wish,
instead of almond milk, take sweet cream of cows.

# A ÐISh FLAVOREÐ WITh ROSE PETALS

During the stormy years after the fall of the Roman
Empire, nearly all knowledge of horticulture died out.
Only those plants thoroughly acclimatized to England
were hardy enough to grow when not properly cultivated. One such hardy plant was a species of the rose.

If you use fresh flowers for this pudding, please be
sure they have not been sprayed with harmful insecti-
cides. Similar recipes call for violets, primroses, and
hawthorn flowers; you may wish to substitute one of
these. If you use fresh flowers, double the amount
indicated.

Eaten alone, *rosee* is rather heavy and rich. You
may wish to fold it into a cup of whipped cream, use it
as a topping for vanilla ice cream, or spread it between
the layers of a white cake.

¹/₂ cup dried, crushed rose petals
3 cups almond milk (see recipe, p. 116)
¹/₂ teaspoon cinnamon
¹/₄ teaspoon powdered ginger
2 teaspoons rice flour
1 cup minced dates
3 tablespoons pine nuts
dash salt (optional)
optional garnish: fresh rose petals

1. Soak rose petals in almond milk for about 10 minutes.
2. Add cinnamon and ginger, and cook 3 to 5 minutes over low heat.
3. Add rice flour and stir until thickened.
4. Add dates and pine nuts.
5. Pour into individual custard cups or small bowl. Chill.
6. Just before serving, sprinkle with a dash of salt if you wish.
7. Garnish with fresh rose petals, if you like, or follow one of the suggestions opposite.

SERVES 6–8

*Sambocade*   Take and make a crust in a trape and take a cruddes and wryng out the wheyze and drawe hem thurgh a stynor. And put in the stynor crustes. Do thereto sugar, the thridde part and somdel whyte of ayren and shake thereinne blomes of elren, and bake it up with curose and messe it forth.

*Elderflower Cheesecake*   Take and make a pie crust in a pie plate and take curds and wring out the wheys and draw them through a strainer. And put crusts in the strainer [i.e., make them into bread crumbs]. Add sugar, one-third the amount of curds, and some egg whites, and shake in blossoms of elderflower and bake it with care and send it forth in portions.

# ELDERFLOWER CHEESECAKE

The name *sambocade* is derived from the Latin word for elderflowers: *sambucus*. The flowers add a pleasing aroma and taste, both of which are difficult to describe. Use a butter-based pie crust and serve this sweet cheesecake warm for optimum flavor and texture. If you wish to substitute fresh elderflowers, double the amount indicated. Be sure you do not collect them from roadsides, as they may contain lead from gasoline fumes.

> 9-inch uncooked pie pastry
> 3 tablespoons dried elderflowers
> 4 tablespoons heavy cream
> $1/_3$ cup sugar
> $1/_2$ pound farmers cheese
> $1/_2$ pound ricotta cheese
> 2 teaspoons dry bread crumbs
> 6 egg whites, beaten until stiff but not dry

1. Bake pie pastry at 425° for 10 minutes. Let cool.
2. Soak elderflowers in heavy cream for about 10 minutes.
3. Add sugar and stir until dissolved.
4. Push cheeses through a strainer with the back of a tablespoon.
5. Combine cheeses with elderflower-cream mixture. Add bread crumbs. Blend thoroughly.
6. Fold in stiff egg whites.
7. Pour mixture into pastry crust.
8. Bake at 375° about 50 minutes or until firm but not dry. Turn off heat and allow to cool in oven with door open about 15 minutes.

SERVES 8

*Crustade Lombarde* Take gode creme, and levys of Percely, and Eyroun, the yolkys and the whyte, and breke hem ther-to, and strayne thorwe a straynoure tyl it be so styf that it wol bere hym-self. Than take fayre Marwe and Datys y-cutte in ij or iij and Prunes and putte the Datys an the Prunes and Marwe on a fayre Cofynne y-mad of fayre past and put the cofyn on the oven tyl it be a lytel hard. Thanne draw hem out of the oven. Take the lycour and putte ther-on and fylle it uyppe and caste Sugre y-now on, and if it be in lente, let the Eyroun and the Marwe out and thanne serve it forth.

*Lombardy Custard* Take good cream and leaves of parsley and eggs, the yolks and the whites, and break them into the cream. Beat the mixture until it is so stiff that it will stand by itself. Then take fresh marrow and dates cut into two or three, and prunes, and put the dates and the prunes and the marrow into a fair coffin made of fair paste, and put the coffin into the oven until it is a little hard. Then draw it out of the oven. Take the liquid and put it into the coffin and fill it up and cast enough sugar on. If it is Lent, leave the eggs and marrow out, and then serve it forth.

# LOMBARDY CUSTARD

This recipe for *Crustade Lombarde* is from the Harleian Manuscript 4016. The spicy fruited custard was served at King Richard's feast given with the Duke of Lancaster on September 23, 1387. It is one of my favorite medieval dishes and always makes a hit with guests. The marrow adds a rich and delicate flavor, and the sweetness of the dried fruits is contrasted in an unusual way with fresh parsley.

> 9-inch uncooked pie pastry
> 10 each prunes, dates, and dried figs, cut into small pieces
> 2 tablespoons raw bone marrow, crumbled*
> 3 tablespoons finely minced parsley
> 1 cup heavy cream
> 2 tablespoons brown sugar
> 2 eggs, lightly beaten
> pinch salt
> 3/4 teaspoon dried orange peel
> 1 teaspoon cinnamon
> pinch mace

1. Bake pie pastry at 425° for 10 minutes. Let cool.
2. Line pie crust with dried fruits. Distribute marrow and parsley evenly over fruit.
3. Combine remaining ingredients in a bowl. Beat until thoroughly blended. Pour over fruits in crust.
4. Bake at 375° for about 20 minutes or until custard is set and top is brown.
5. Let the *crustade* cool about 5 minutes before serving.

SERVES 8

* Ask your butcher to hack open a beef bone so that you can easily get at the marrow.

**Autumpne comith ayein hevy of apples.**

CHAUCER
*Boethius* (c. 1382)

*Appulmoy* Take apples and seeth hem in water. Drawe hem
thurgh a stynnor. Take almande mylke and hony and floer of
rys, safron, and powdor-fort, and salt, and seeth it stondyng.

*Applesauce* Take apples and boil them in water. Push them
through a strainer. Take almond milk, honey, rice flour, saffron, strong spice, and salt, and cook it to a stiff consistency.

# Applesauce

"Apples strengthen the heart," says a medieval treatise on hygiene, "especially those that have a nice smell."* Here is an unusually flavored applesauce with the crunchy texture of almonds.

> 2 1/2 pounds apples, quartered and cored but unpeeled
> 1 cup water
> 1/2 cup unstrained almond milk (see p. 116)
> 1/2 teaspoon cinnamon
> 1/8–1/4 teaspoon powdered ginger
> 1/4 teaspoon saffron
> 8 crushed cubebs
> pinch each cardamom, mace, salt
> 3 teaspoons rice flour dissolved in 1 tablespoon water (optional)

1. Simmer apples in water in a covered pan about 10 minutes or until they are easily pierced with a knife.
2. Strain through fine sieve of a food mill and return pulp to pan.
3. Add remaining ingredients (except rice flour).
4. Cook over low heat, stirring constantly. If additional thickness is desired, add rice flour dissolved in water.
5. Serve hot or cold.

YIELD: about 3 cups

* Way, p. 33.

She was wel more blisful on to see
Than is the newe perjente tree.

CHAUCER
"Miller's Tale" (c. 1386)

*Peeres in Confyt*   Take peeres and pare hem clene. Take gode rede wyne and mulberes other sandres and seeth the peers thereinne. And whan their buth isode take hem up. Make a syrup of wyne greke or vernage with blanche powdor other white sugar and powdor gynger and do the peeres therein. Seeth it a lytel and messe it forth.

*Pears in Confection*   Take pears and trim them clean. Take good red wine and mulberries or sandalwood and boil the pears in it. And when they are cooked, take them out. Make a syrup of Greek wine or Vernaccia with white powder or white sugar and powdered ginger and put the pears in it. Boil it a little and serve it forth.

# pears in confection

The pear existed in numerous varieties in the Middle Ages. The pear-jenet mentioned by Chaucer was an early-ripening pear. Most recipes call for Wardens, an old variety of baking pear.

Sandalwood turns the pears a dark red and gives them an unusually pleasant flavor. Mulberries may be substituted as a coloring and flavoring agent.

This dish was served at Henry IV's wedding feast.

> 6 large firm cooking pears, peeled, cut in half, and cored
> 2 cups water or red wine
> $1/_2$ teaspoon red sandalwood powder
> 1 $1/_2$ cups good-quality Muscatel, Vernaccia, or any sweet heavy wine
> $1/_2$–$3/_4$ teaspoon powdered ginger
> 2 tablespoons confectioner's sugar (or more for thicker syrup)
> garnish: pomegranate seeds

1. Boil pears in the water or red wine and sandalwood in a covered pot about 15 minutes or until soft but still firm. Drain.
2. Combine sweet wine, ginger, and sugar. Bring to a boil and cook until syrup is slightly reduced and thickened.
3. Pour syrup over pears. Serve warm or cold, garnished with pomegranate seeds.

SERVES 6

# MISCELLANEOUS

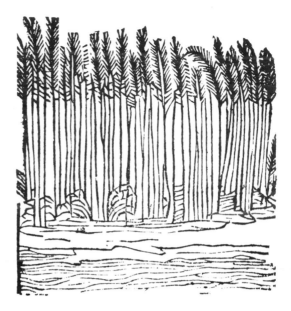

*Brede and Rastons*  Take fayre Flowre and the whyte of Eyroun and the yolke, a lytel. Than take Warme Berme, and putte al thes to-gederys and bete hem to-gederys with thin hond tyl it be schort and thikke y-now, and caste Sugre y-now ther-to, and thenne lat reste a whyle. An kaste in a fayre place in the oven and late bake y-now. And then with a knyf cutte yt round a-bove in maner of a crowne, and kepe the crust that thou kyttest, and than caste ther-in clarifiyd Boter and Mille the cromes and the botere to-gederes, and kevere it a-yen with the cruste that thou kyttest a-way. Than putte it in the ovyn ayen a lytil tyme and than take it out, and serve it forth.

*Bread and Stuffed Loaves*  Take good flour, egg white, and a little yolk. Then take warm barm. Put these all together and beat them with your hand until the dough is crumbly and dense. Add enough sugar and then let it rest a while. Cast it into a good spot in the oven and let it bake enough. Then with a knife, cut into the top crust in the shape of a crown and keep the crusts that you've cut. Put clarified butter inside and stir the crumbs and the butter together. Cover it again with the crust that you cut away. Then put it in the oven again for a little time. Then take it out and serve it forth.

112

# BREAD AND STUFFED LOAVES

Harleian Manuscript 279, the source of the recipe opposite, is the only large collection of recipes which contains a bread recipe, probably because the cookery books were dictated to scribes by cooks and not bakers. Warm ale barm was used instead of yeast in the Middle Ages. Since the fermentation process of our bottled ale has been halted, we must add yeast to the ingredients.

The following recipe was developed by comparing the instructions opposite with the description for preparing manchet loaves on page 17. Since most medieval flour wasn't bleached white, you may wish to give your bread a more natural look by blending a half-cup of whole wheat flour with the unbleached. As whole wheat flour tends to absorb more moisture than white, you will probably find that you need slightly less flour overall.

This recipe, since it tells us to take *fayre Flowre*, is for bread to be eaten at the table. Trenchers were made of inferior flour, probably rye and whole wheat, and you may wish to experiment with these to make bread plates for a feast. But don't forget to make them four days in advance so they can get sufficiently hard.

TO MAKE THE BREAD

> 3 packages dry yeast
> $^1/_2$ cup warm water
> 1 $^1/_2$ cups ale at room temperature
> 2 tablespoons sugar
> 1 tablespoon salt
> 1 egg, lightly beaten
> 5–6 cups unbleached flour
> 2 tablespoons milk (optional)

1. Dissolve yeast in warm water.
2. Combine ale, yeast solution, sugar, salt, and egg in a large bowl.

3. Add 4 cups of flour and blend ingredients by stirring with a large spoon.
4. Turn dough onto a floured board and begin to knead it (follow the instructions for kneading in a basic cookbook; it is essential that kneading be done correctly if the bread is to have the proper texture).
5. As you knead, work in an additional 1 to 2 cups of flour by sprinkling it on the top before folding the dough over. Stop adding flour when the dough loses its stickiness.
6. Knead about 12 minutes, or until smooth and elastic.
7. Place dough mass into a bowl. Cover it with a moistened cloth and set it in a warm place for one hour or until doubled in bulk.
8. Punch down dough by socking your fist into it 25 to 30 times.
9. Divide it into two or four portions. Shape each portion into a round loaf, and place the loaves on a greased cookie sheet. Score the top twice; make about eight diagonal slashes around the perimeter to encourage bread to rise while baking.
10. If you wish top crusts to turn golden, brush them with milk.
11. Bake in a preheated 375° oven about 30 minutes. When it is done, the bread should sound hollow when you knock the top.

YIELD: 2 large or 4 small round loaves

TO MAKE RASTONS

The medieval concern for appearance and a bit of magic is apparent here. The loaf is meant to look untouched when served, so that the flavored stuffing will come as a pleasing surprise to the eater. Their butter probably had more impurities than ours; thus, the suggestion to clarify it.

How were rastons served? You'll probably find that any way you slice it, the bread will be crumbly.

1 large round loaf white bread

$^1/_2$ cup lightly salted butter (clarified, if you wish)

1 tablespoon poppy or crushed fennel seeds (optional)

1. With an up-down motion of the knife, cut top crust off in the shape of a flattened crown (the zigzag shape we usually associate with cutting off the top of a pumpkin).
2. Carefully lift off the crust and set it aside.
3. Scoop out the bread and crumble.
4. Melt butter in a heavy skillet.
5. Toss crumbs in butter until they are evenly coated.
6. Mix with poppy or fennel seeds if you wish.
7. Replace buttered crumbs in loaf and put top crust back in place.
8. Reheat in moderate oven (350°) for a few minutes before serving.

SERVES 4–6

## Von Souris

**Almon mylk . . . doth mollyfe the bely.**

BOORDE,
*Dyetary* (1542)

*Cold Mylk of Almondes*  To mak cold mylk of almondes put fair water in a pot with sugar or honey clarified so that it be douce. Then salt it and set it on the fyere and when it is at boilling scom and let it boile awhile. Then tak it from the fyere and let it kele. Then blanche youre almondes and grind them, and temper them with the same water in to a good thik mylk, and put it to wyne that it may have a good flavour ther of, and serve it. Then cut bred and toist it and baist it and toist it again that it be hard and serve them in one disshe and the mylk in any other disshe.

*Cold Almond Milk*  To make cold milk of almonds put good water in a pot with sugar or clarified honey so that it will be sweet. Then salt it and set it on the fire and when it is boiling skim it and let it boil a while. Then take it from the fire and let it cool. Then blanch your almonds and grind them and mix them with the same water into a good thick milk. Add wine so it may have a good flavor and serve it. Then cut bread and toast it and baste it and toast it again so it is hard, and serve the bread in one dish and the milk in another dish.

# COLÐ ALMONÐ MiLk

One of the most popular ingredients in medieval cookery, almond milk was used as a thickener and flavoring agent in a wide variety of meat and fruit dishes. It was also served hot or cold as a dip for making sops of toasted bread. Almond milk was apparently so commonly known that few cooks bothered to write the recipe down. The above instructions are therefore extremely valuable as the only published source known.*

* The recipe is found in a rare manuscript (c. 1467) in the Holkham collection. It is printed in Mrs. Alexander Napier, *A Noble Boke off Cookry ffor a Prynce houssolde* (London, 1882).

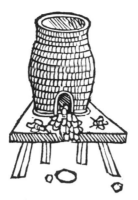

Almonds may be steeped in heated broth or wine rather than in boiling water.

   $^1/_2$ **cup blanched almonds (see directions below)**
   **ice water**
   **1 cup boiling water**
   **$1^1/_2$ teaspoons honey**
   **dash salt**

1. To blanch almonds, boil the nuts in water for 2 to 3 minutes. Drain. Pour cold water over them. Pop off the skins.
2. Grind almonds in blender or mortar, adding a few tablespoons of ice water during the process to prevent the paste from becoming oily. If you enjoy a crunchy texture, leave them coarse; otherwise pulverize them.
3. Add honey and salt to 1 cup boiling water and dissolve.
4. Pour liquid over almonds. Allow to soak about 10 minutes, stirring occasionally.
5. Strain out almonds if a smooth texture is desired.
6. Store in refrigerator and use as needed. Will last about 3 days.

   YIELD: $1^1/_4$ cups unstrained; 1 cup strained

**Loke your composte be fayre and clene.**

*Boke of Kervyng* (1513)

*Compost* Take rote of parsel, pasternak of rasens. Scrape hem and waisshe hem clene. Take rapes and caboches ypared and icorne. Take an earthen pane with clene water, and set it on the fire. Cast all thise thereinne. Whan they buth boiled, cast thereto peeres and parboile hem wele. Take thise thynges up, and lat it kele on a fair cloth. Do thereto salt, whan it is colde, in a vessel. Take vynegar and powdor and safron and do thereto. And lat alle thise thynges lye thereinne al nygt other al day. Take wyne greke and hony clarified togider, lumbarde mustard, and raisons, corance al hool and grynde powdor of canal, powdor douce and aneys hole, and fenell seed. Take alle thise thynges and cast togyder in a pot of erthe and take thereof whan thou wilt and serve it forth.

*Preserved Fruits and Vegetables* Take parsley root and carefully raised [?] parsnips. Scrape them and wash them clean. Take turnips pared and cabbages cut into pieces. Take an earthenware pot and set it on the fire. Cast all these things into it. When they are boiled, add pears and parboil them well. Take these things out and cool them on a good cloth. Add salt and put the mixture into a vessel when it is cold. Take vinegar and powdered spices and saffron and add them. And let all these things lie together all night or all day. Take Greek wine and clarified honey mixed, Lombardy mustard, raisins, and whole currants. Grind powder of cinnamon, sweet powder, whole aniseed, and fennel seed. Take all these things and cast them together into an earthenware pot and take from it whenever you wish and serve it forth.

# pRESERVEĐ FRUiTS
# ANĐ VEGETAbLES

The word *compost* in Middle English meant a combination of various ingredients—often, but not always, what we think of today as compote. Here is a sweet and pungent dish served as a potage at a fifteenth-century feast given by Lord Grey. We would be more likely to consider it a pickled relish.

4 cups water
$^1/_2$ teaspoon salt
$^1/_4$ head of cabbage, sliced into thin strips or
    coarsely shredded
$^1/_2$ pound small turnips, peeled and minced
3 parsley roots, scraped and cubed (optional)
3 parsnips, scraped and cubed
2 pears, peeled, cored, and cubed
1 cup Muscatel
$^1/_2$ cup wine vinegar
1 tablespoon honey
$^1/_4$ teaspoon saffron
$^1/_4$ teaspoon cinnamon
$^1/_2$ teaspoon whole cloves
2 thin slices of peeled fresh ginger
$^1/_2$ teaspoon each coarsely crushed aniseed,
    fennel seed, mustard seed, and cubebs
$^1/_4$ cup currants and raisins

1. Bring water and salt to a boil in a four-quart porcelain casserole.
2. Add vegetables. Reduce flame and cook covered about 5 minutes.
3. Add the pears and cook an additional 10 minutes or until all ingredients are soft but firm.
4. Drain vegetables and pears in a colander and set aside.
5. In the top of a double boiler, combine wine, vinegar, and honey.
6. Heat to just boiling and add saffron and cinnamon, stirring until blended.
7. Return vegetables and pears to the porcelain pot and pour the syrup over them, stirring until all of the solids are coated.
8. Prepare a bouquet garni by wrapping the cloves, ginger, aniseed, fennel seed, mustard seed, and cubebs in a small piece of doubled cheesecloth, tying the top with string or a rubber band.

9. Drop the bouquet garni into the mixture. Add the currants and raisins, stirring to distribute them evenly.
10. Allow to stand a few hours, stirring occasionally.
11. Refrigerate overnight before serving.
12. Remove bouquet garni and serve rewarmed or cold.

YIELD: 2–3 cups

**Sit and ete the cawdel . . . that was made with sugir and with swete wyne.**

*Tale of Beryn* (c. 1400)

*Cawdel Ferry* Take flour of payndemayn and gode wyne and drawe it togydre. Do thereto a grete quantite of sugar cypre, or hony clarified and do thereto safronn. Boile it and whan it is boiled, alye it up with yolkes of ayren, and do thereto salt, and messe it forth and lay thereto sugar and powdor gynger.

*Warm Thick Gruel* Take the flour of fine white bread and good wine and steep them together. Add a great quantity of sugar of Cyprus, or clarified honey and saffron. Boil it, and when it has boiled, add egg yolks and salt. Divide it into portions and sprinkle sugar and powdered ginger on top.

# WARM Thick GRUeL

This creamy gruel was often served as a healing drink to the sick. It goes down easily, like warm milk and honey. Make it with your favorite wine.

> 1 cup wine
> ¼ cup finely ground crumbs from fine-quality white bread or pound cake
> 1 teaspoon honey or sugar (or to taste)
> ⅛ teaspoon saffron
> pinch salt
> 1 egg yolk, lightly beaten
> pinch ginger and sugar

1. Combine wine, crumbs, honey or sugar, saffron, and salt in the top of a double boiler. Cook over a medium flame, stirring to blend.
2. As soon as the mixture starts to boil, remove it from the flame.
3. Beat a few tablespoons of hot liquid into beaten egg yolk.
4. Add remaining wine mixture and stir.
5. Pour into a mug and sprinkle ginger and sugar on top before drinking.

SERVES 1

He drynketh Ypocras, Clarree and Vernage of spices
hoote tencressen [to increase] his corage.

CHAUCER
"Merchant's Tale" (c. 1386)

*Pur Fait Ypocras*   Treys unces de canell et iij unces de gyn-
gener, spykenard de spayn le pays dun denerer, garyngale,
clowes, gylofre, pocurer long, noiez mugadez, maziozame,
cardomonii de chescun j quarter douce, grayne & de paradys,
floer de queynel, de chescun di unce. De toutes fait powdor,
& c.

*To Make Hippocras*   The above recipe is written in a very
corrupt fourteenth-century French and may have been copied
from a contemporary French manuscript. It is the only recipe
in the *Forme of Cury* which uses this dialect. What follows is
more a paraphrase than a translation:

Take three ounces each of cinnamon and ginger and take
spikenard of Spain the size of a small coin. Take one quarter of
an ounce each of galingale, cloves, long pepper, nutmeg, and
cardamom. Take an ounce of grains of paradise and of powdered cinnamon and make powders of all. . . .

# TO MAKE HIPPOCRAS

We are told in some detail about the process of making
this spiced wine in John Russell's *Boke of Nurture*
(see Furnivall). The section is too long to be reproduced in the original. Here is a translated synopsis:

Have three pewter basins for the liquid and three strain-
ing bags, one for each, hanging inside of them from a
perch. Pare ginger or beat it into a powder and be sure to
use the columbine variety. Your cinnamon sticks should
be thin, brittle, and fair in color. Use grains of paradise,
sugar, red wine, long pepper and turnsole for coloring.
Put each spice into a separate bladder and hang these bags
from the perch so that they don't touch each other. Place
two or three gallons of wine into each of the basins. Allow
the wine to absorb the flavors from the spice pouches.
Then strain the liquid through the long cloth bag called a
Hippocrate's sleeve. Taste it. If there is too much ginger,
add cinnamon, and vice versa. After you have made hippocras, you can use the spice dregs in the kitchen.

In the words of the old master himself:

> "Now, good son, thine ypocras is made parfite and welle y wold [I know]. Than ye put it in staunche and a clene vessclle, and the mouthe ther-off y-stopped ever more wisely and felle, and serve hit forth with wafurs bothe in chambur and Celle."

If you don't wish to follow John Russell's elaborate instructions for making *ypocras*, try this recipe:

1 bottle Burgundy wine
$1/4$ cup sugar
4 sticks cinnamon, broken into pieces
3 thin slices fresh ginger
1 teaspoon whole cloves
5 cardamom pods, coarsely crushed
$1/8$ teaspoon grains of paradise, finely ground
a few pieces of fresh orange or lemon peel

1. Combine above ingredients in an enamel pan.
2. Bring to a boil; then reduce flame and simmer about 15 minutes, stirring occasionally.
3. Strain liquid to remove whole spices if you wish.
4. Serve warm in goblets or shallow bowls.

SERVES 4

# PLANNING
# THE MEDIEVAL FEAST

Aprofessor once told me that the quickest way out of Manhattan is to open a volume of the *Canterbury Tales*. With as much ease and as little expense, your feast can be set in an atmosphere suggestive of medieval England.

Light the dining room with large candles and play recordings of medieval music in the background. Balance a door on carpenter's horses for a groaning board, and cover your table with a cloth. Set each place with a napkin, spoon, knife, trencher, and goblet or mazer cup (a small, shallow bowl will do). Place the salt and spices in small dishes around the table.

Suggest that your guests wear costumes of the period. After they have been seated, place a small portion of every type of food on each trencher. Serve sauces in small bowls placed between each couple and advise them either to dip meat into the sauce or spoon the liquid onto their portions. Encourage diners to use their hands for eating those foods which cannot comfortably be lifted in a spoon. Request that guests use the pinky finger for taking spices; etiquette requires that these "spice fingers" be held in a raised position while eating to keep them free of grease.

Pass around a towel and large bowl of warm water scented with aromatic spices before the meal and between courses so that guests may wash their hands. When a trencherman raises a piece of roast goose to his lips, he will find that the lingering scent of the water will enhance the food's flavor.

If you are not able to make your own trenchers, you will find that the pizza bread sold in most Italian neighborhoods is an excellent substitute. Cut each loaf in half horizontally across the middle, square off the edges of each half, and you will have two trenchers. Try to buy the bread a few days before your feast to allow time for hardening, and be sure to have a few extras for those guests who dig too deeply and end up with leaky bread plates. In the Middle Ages, used trenchers were given as alms to the poor. But if your guests have enjoyed their adventure with medieval cuisine, do not be surprised to find that the sauce-sopped trencher has been consumed along with the rest of the meal.

## The Menu

During a medieval feast, guests consumed the equivalent of three complete meals in a row. Since we are no longer accustomed to eating for the better part of a day, today's cook might create the impression of variety and abundance by preparing many dishes in small quantities and advising guests to sample food rather than take normal portions.

To plan a feast menu, consider the principal ingredients in each recipe; then choose dishes according to the order and combinations you normally enjoy. Check to be sure you are not duplicating certain foods. For example, you would not wish to serve *Tart de Brymlent* as an entrée with *Leshes Fryed in Lenton* for dessert, nor would *Sawse Madame* provide sufficient contrast to either.

Most of the dishes are flavored with compatible spices, and you will find that they complement each other rather nicely. But since many people are not accustomed to the sweetness characteristic of the cuisine, set off your main dishes with a salad, something pungent (such as *Gele of Fysshe* or a vinegary sauce), or a vegetable seasoned primarily with salt and pepper (see *Funges* or *Aquapatys*).

Serve dry red or white wine during the meal and *Ypocras* after dinner.

*Suggested Menus*

### FEAST FOR FOUR

| Tartlettes | | Gele of Fysshe |
|---|---|---|
| | Salat | |
| | Douce Ame | |
| Funges | | Fritors of Apples |
| | Sambocade | |
| | Ypocras | |

### FEAST FOR TEN

| Gourdes in Potage | | Gele of Fysshe |
|---|---|---|
| | Salat | |
| Connynges in Cyrip | | Tartee |
| Aquapatys | | Fritors of Parsnip |
| | Leshes Fryed in Lenton | |
| | Ypocras | |

### FEAST FOR TWENTY

Muskels in Brewet     Tart de Bry

Salat

Roo Broth    Tart de Brymlent    Blank-mang

Aquapatys    Funges    Fritors of Parsnips

Crustade Lombarde    Sambocade

Ypocras

# GLOSSARY OF INGREDIENTS

**alkanet**  a group of plants whose roots give off a red dye; used primarily as a coloring agent, but according to some early herbalists, "it helps old ulcers, hot inflammations, and burnings by common fire."

**almond milk**  a cloudy liquid prepared by steeping ground almonds in water, broth, or wine; acts as the liquid base and/or thickening agent in a wide variety of medieval dishes. Its medicinal values are praised by Boorde, who claims that "it doth comforte the brest, and it doth mollyfye the bely, and provoketh uryne."

**avens**  the herb was used in salads and the root to impart a clovelike flavor to ale. Avens was considered "the blessed herb," and according to the *Ortus Sanitatus* (Garden of Health), printed in 1491, "If a man carries the root [of avens] about him, no venemous beast can harm him."

**barm**  the foamy yeast that appears on the top of malt liquors as they ferment; ale barm was commonly used as the yeast element in breads and batters.

**bittern**  a heronlike wading bird.

**blaunderelle**  a variety of white apple. According to Boorde, apples "doth comforte the stomacke, and doth make good dygestyon, specyally yf they be rostyd or baken."

**borage**  a blue-flowered plant with hairy leaves that taste somewhat like cucumber; used primarily in salads. "Borage," Boorde says, "doth comforte the herte, and doth ingender good blode, and causeth a man to be mery."

**bream** a European fresh-water fish related to the carp; any of various salt-water fishes, as the sea bream.

**bullace** a purple wild plum.

**calver salmon** exact meaning unknown; possibly refers to the fresh salmon sliced and prepared in a special way, perhaps pickled.

**chamomile** any of several plants of the aster family, with scented leaves and small daisylike flowers; the dried leaves and flowers were used in herbal cures, and Boorde recommends rubbing the body with oil of chamomile to cure palsy.

**chibol** a type of small onion no longer cultivated; substitute scallions or shallots when making *salat*.

**chickweed** a weed with juicy stems and small white flowers; the juice of chickweed was drunk to heal cramps, convulsions, and palsies.

**clarified honey** honey whose impurities have been forced to the top by boiling and removed by skimming. Many medieval recipes recommend clarifying honey by combining it with wine. As the wine fermented, a scum formed on top and the liquid became clear.

**clary** a plant of the sage family which cuts the grease of fatty meats and fish; in the late Middle Ages, its name was thought to mean "clair-ye" (clear eye) and ointments prepared with the herb were believed to sharpen vision The early clary wine, a white wine so named for its clarity, is the etymological ancestor of our modern claret.

**codling** a young or small cod, perhaps salted; Furnivall notes that "ling" may be a corruption of "lying" in salt.

**coffin** a mold of pastry for a pie.

**confection** the sugar paste in which whole spices were dipped; confectioned spices were used as garnishes and eaten at the end of feasts, to aid digestion.

**cubeb** a berry from Java which resembles a peppercorn and tastes somewhat like allspice; its special aromatic flavor cannot be duplicated, but a blend of half pepper and half allspice may serve as a substitute.

**curlew** a large brownish wading bird.

**cygnet** a young swan.

**damson** sometimes called bullace, this bluish black plum is named for the place of its origin, Damascus; damson preserves or plums of any variety may be used as a substitute.

**dittany** a plant of the mint family with oval leaves and clusters of purplish flowers; the pungent, aromatic leaves were used in salads and as a medicinal herb. The application of dittany combined with black soap was thought to aid in the extraction of "splint, iron, thorne or stub."

**dotterel** the European plover, a short-billed shore bird.

**egret** a heron with long white plumes.

**farce** stuffing; after the Middle Ages became the generic term for short dramatic pieces "stuffed" with buffoonery.

**galingale** an aromatic root; the main ingredient of **galyntyne**, a pungent medieval sauce. Boorde recommends galingale to "comforte the stomake." Galingale is available in powdered form at shops which specialize in Indonesian spices.

**good powders** potent ground spices.

**grains of paradise** the aromatic pungent seeds of a tropical West African plant. Boorde says, "Graynes be good for the stomake and the head." Grains are related to cardamom, which may be used as a substitute.

**Greek wine** a generic term which relates to any sweet full-bodied wine.

**gudgeon** a small European fresh-water fish of the carp family.

**gurnard** a spiny-finned sea fish having a large head and wing-like pectoral fins.

**hake** any of various edible sea fishes resembling or related to the cod.

**hyssop** a blue-flowered plant of the mint family whose leaves cut the grease in fatty meats and fish. According to one medieval treatise, "when eaten it improves weak sight, relieves asthma, and expels worms, but causes miscarriage."

**lamprey** any of a group of eellike water animals with a funnel-shaped, jawless, sucking mouth; also called lamper eel.

**laver** an edible purple seaweed; available dry in organic and Oriental food shops.

**loach** a small European fresh-water fish of the carp family.

**Lombardy mustard** a paste prepared by combining ground mustard seed with honey, wine, and vinegar.

**marlin** any of several large, slender deep-sea fishes related to the sailfish and spearfish.

**medlar**  a small, brown, applelike fruit, hard and bitter when ripe and eaten only when partly decayed.

**orach**  a garden plant with red or green leaves used as a vegetable and a salad herb.

**pellitory**  a climbing plant of the nettle family whose leaves were used in salads and roots for medicinal cures. According to one herbalist, pellitory "is one of the best purges of the brain that grows . . . and an excellent remedy in lethargy."

**plover**  a shore bird with a short tail, long pointed wings, and brown or gray feathers mixed with white.

**porret**  a young leek or onion; a scallion.

**powder**  ground spice.

**purslane**  a plant with a pinkish fleshy stem and small, round leaves; the leaves were used as a potherb or in salads. Boorde informs us that "purslane dothe extynct the ardor of lassyvyousnes, and doth mytygate great heate in all the in warde partes of man."

**rail**  a small wading bird resembling the crane.

**ramson**  a kind of garlic with broad leaves; the root was used in salads.

**rayfish**  a fish with a horizontally flat body, both eyes on the upper surface, and a slender, whiplike tail.

**roach**  a fresh-water fish of the carp family.

**rocket**  mildly pungent plant grown like spinach and eaten in salads. According to Boorde, rocket "doth increase the seede of man, and doth stimulate the flesshe, and doth helpe to dygestyon." Also known as arugula.

**rose hips**  the fleshy, bright-colored fruit of the rose plant; rose hips have a tart taste and are known today as an excellent source of vitamin C.

**rue**  a plant with yellow flowers whose bitter-tasting leaves were used mostly in herbal cures but occasionally in salads. Gerard notes that "the juice of Rue made hot in the rinde of a pomegranat and dropped into the eares, takes away the pain of [sic] thereof."

**St.-John's-wort**  a plant with brownish stalks and small, narrow leaves; the latter were used in salads and pounded into oil for healing wounds. The seeds have such a resinous odor, it was believed that if evil spirits were to take a whiff of it, they would be driven away.

**sandalwood**  the pulverized wood of an East Indian tree used primarily to color food dark red.

**skirret**  a species of water parsnip not available in this country and no longer cultivated on a large scale in Europe. Gerard declares that "these roots [may] be eaten boiled, with vinegar, salt, and a little oyle, after the manner of a sallad, and oftentimes they be fried in oyle and butter, and also dressed after other fashions, according to the skill of the cooke, and the taste of the eater."

**snipe**  a wading bird which lives in marshy places and is characterized by a long, flexible bill.

**southernwood**  a shrubby fragrant plant with yellowish flowers and bitter-tasting leaves; it was used both as a culinary herb and in medicinal cures. "Boiled in barley meal it taketh away pimples," claims an early herbalist.

**spikenard**  an aromatic plant of northern India whose root was used in the preparation of medicinal ointments for curing bruises; the very smell of the plant was said to destroy fleas.

**strong powder (pouder fort)**  probably ground ginger or a blend of cinnamon and mace; the blend may have included any of the pungent spices such as cubeb, pepper, or clove.

**sweet powder (pouder douce)**  probably the ground sweet aromatic spices such as aniseed, fennel seed, and nutmeg; there is no indication that these spices were blended with sugar.

**tansy**  a bitter medicinal herb whose juice was traditionally extracted from the young leaves, mixed with eggs, and baked as a "tansy cake" (or simply a "tansy"). These cakes were thought to purify the body and were often eaten after Lent to counteract the effects of fasting fare.

**teal**  any of a large group of small, short-necked, fresh-water ducks.

**tench**  a European fresh-water fish of the carp family.

**turnsole**  a plant cultivated primarily for its use as a purple dye.

**verjuice**  the juice of green or unripened fruits such as grapes and (more commonly) crab apples; a popular ingredient in cookery which often replaced vinegar. A medieval source gives instructions for making verjuice: "Gather crabbs as soon as the kernels turn blacke, and lay them in a heap to sweat and take them into troughs and crush with beetles [heavy wooden mallets]. Make a bagge of coarse hair-cloth and fill it with the crabbes, and presse and run the liquor into Hogsheads." You might experiment with rose hip syrup (available at health food stores) as a substitute.

**Vernaccia**   Vernage, a strong sweet Italian wine; Muscatel or any other sweet heavy wine may be substituted.

**vervain**   a medicinal plant of the verbena family, slightly bitter in taste. The name *vervain* is derived from the Celtic *ferfaen*, from *fer* (to drive away) and *faen* (a stone), as the plant was much used to soothe attacks of the bladder.

**Warden**   a hard pear with blackish bruises; prepared by baking or stewing.

**whelk**   a large marine snail with a spiral shell.

**white grease**   lard.

**white powder (blanch pouder)**   ground ginger blended with powdered sugar.

**woodcock**   a small migratory game bird related to the snipe and sandpiper.

**wormwood**   a strong-smelling plant with white or yellow flowers used in the Middle Ages as an aid to healthful digestion; the expression "as bitter as wormwood" attests to the extreme bitterness of all parts of the plant.

# SOURCES FOR INGREDIENTS

Unless otherwise noted, all will accept mail order.

## Dried Herbs and Spices

**Aphrodisia**
28 Carmine Street
New York, New York 10014

**Attar**
Smith Village
New Ipswich, New Hampshire 03071

**Butterfly Herbs**
515 South Higgins Avenue
Missoula, Montana 59801

**Coffees of the World**
4573 University Avenue
San Diego, California 92105

**Flavorworld**
622 St. Ann Street
New Orleans, Louisiana 70116

**Homecrafts**
111 Stratford Center
Winston-Salem, North Carolina 27104

**House of Hezekiah**
504 Walnut
Kansas City, Missouri 64106

**The Rosemary House**
120 South Market Street
Mechanicsburg, Pennsylvania 17055

**Star Herb Company**
352 Miller Avenue
Mill Valley, California 94941

# Fresh Herbs and Seeds

**Rutland Herbs**
P.O. Box 583
Georgetown, Kentucky 40324

# Fresh and Frozen Game

**Maryland Gourmet Mart**
1072 First Avenue
New York, New York 10022

**Mickey Houston Foods**
79 South Water Market
Chicago, Illinois 60608

**The Willowbrook 1680 Farm**
Southborough, Massachusetts 01772
(no mail order)

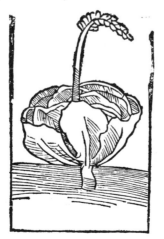

# SUGGESTIONS
# FOR FURTHER
# READING

Amherst, Alicia. *A History of Gardening in England.* London, 1896. Chapters on "Gardens of the Thirteenth and Fourteenth Centuries" and "Early Garden Literature" are important sources of information on plants cultivated in medieval England.

———, ed. "A Fifteenth Century Treatise on Gardening by 'Mayster Ion Gardener.'" *Archaeologia,* 54 (1844), 156–72. A poem on the care of plants and grafting of trees; concludes with a catalog of herbs essential to the medieval English garden.

Boorde, Andrew. *Dyetary.* Ed. F. J. Furnivall. Early English Text Society, e.s. 10. London, 1870. An engaging sixteenth-century treatise on the relationship between food, temperament, and health.

Brett, G. *Dinner Is Served.* Connecticut, 1969. The first half is devoted to a sophisticated and well-documented study of medieval feast manners and table setting; the volume has copious prints and photographs of period art and tableware.

Clair, Colin. *Kitchen and Table.* New York, 1964. A fairly reliable description of food and feast fare in England, with a substantial section on the Middle Ages.

Clarkson, Rosetta. *The Golden Age of Herbs and Herbalists.* Dover paperback, New York, 1972. A popular history of herb gardens and the medicinal uses of herbs.

Drummond, J. C., and Wilbraham, Anne. *The Englishman's Food.* London, 1939. A well-documented survey of food in

England with a lengthy section on the medieval period; special emphasis is on nutritive value of available foods.

Furnivall, F. J., ed. *Early English Meals and Manners*. Early English Text Society, o.s. 32. London, 1868. A scholarly edition of Middle English treatises on courtesy at table and the proper training of a lord's servants; each page has an abridged running translation of the text.

Gerard, John. *Leaves from Gerard's Herball*. Ed. Marcus Woodward. Dover paperback, New York, 1969. An abridged edition of Gerard's *Herball or General Historie of Plantes*, which first appeared in 1597.

Hope, W. H. "On the English Medieval Drinking Bowls called Mazers." *Archaeologia*, 50 (1887), 129–93. This scholarly article by an art historian is particularly valuable for its numerous pictorial illustrations.

Huizinga, Johan. *The Waning of the Middle Ages*. New York, 1954. A provocative study of the ideals, aesthetics, and values of the late Middle Ages.

Labarge, Margaret. *A Baronial Household of the Thirteenth Century*. New York, 1965. A lively, scholarly survey of food and management in a wealthy medieval household.

Loomis, Roger Sherman. *A Mirror of Chaucer's World*. Princeton, 1965. Copious reproductions of period art reveal both daily life and scenes of feasting.

Mathew, Gervase. *The Court of Richard II*. London, 1968. A study of the character of Richard II and his court seen primarily through the great literary artists of the period.

Mead, William. *The English Medieval Feast*. New York, 1967. The only book devoted solely to the subject; it covers the essentials and is a useful place to begin secondary reading.

Pegge, Samuel. *The Forme of Cury*. London, 1780. This edition of the recipes has useful notes and introductory material, but manuscript abbreviations have been maintained and the recipes are difficult to read.

Power, Eileen, trans. *Goodman of Paris*. London, 1928. Written by a Parisian merchant of the fourteenth century to instruct his young wife on cooking and household management, this volume gives a colorful picture of middle-class French life during the period of the *Forme of Cury*.

Pullar, Philippa. *Consuming Passions*. Boston, 1970. A popular history of food in England with a chapter on "Medieval Summer."

Rickert, Edith, ed. *Babees Book*. London, 1908. A reliable modern rendition of the Middle English tracts on courtesy edited by Furnivall in *Early English Meals and Manners*.

Rohde, Eleanour. *The Old English Herbals*. Dover paperback,

New York, 1971. A well-illustrated survey from the Anglo-Saxon period through the seventeenth century; there is an excellent bibliography of manuscript and printed herbals.

Simon, André. *The History of the Wine Trade in England*. Vol. I. London, 1906. Learn about wine and history at the same time.

Warner, Richard. *Antiquitates Culinariae: Tracts on Culinary Affairs of the Old English*. London, 1791. A highly recommended complete edition of the *Forme of Cury* with interesting notes and introduction; also includes an account of the enthronization of Archbishop Neville in 1467 which has detailed instructions on the service of food and responsibilities of household staff.

Way, Arthur, trans. *The Science of Dining: A Medieval Treatise on the Hygiene of the Table*. London, 1936. An entertaining treatise on food, health, and temperament.

Wright, Thomas. *Homes of Other Days*. London, 1971. An excellent volume for background reading on daily life and eating customs from the Anglo-Saxon period to the late Middle Ages.

# iNdex

# NOTES ON THE ILLUSTRATIONS

The banqueters on the cover are from "The Feast of Ahasuerus," an anonymous German woodcut from *Der Spiegel der Menschen Behaltnis*, Speyer, 1479–1481 (Harris Brisbane Dick Fund, 1931). The complete woodcut appears on page 31; details decorate pages 1, 3, 104, and 136.

The wine taster on the cover is a detail from a woodcut, shown in its entirety on page 123, from Petrus de Crescentiis, *Das Buch von Pflanzung der Aecker, Bäume und aller Kräuter*, Strasbourg, 1512 (Harris Brisbane Dick Fund, 1926). All text illustrations come from this source, unless otherwise noted below.

The illustration on page 19 is from a facsimile reproduction in W. L. Schreiber, *Handbuch der Holz- und Metallschnitte des XV. Jahrhunderts*, Leipzig, 1927 (Rogers Fund, 1928). The original fifteenth-century German woodcut is in the Kestner Museum, Hanover.

Pages 3, 37, 83, 101, 127, 133, and 139 are illustrated with woodcuts from Hartmann Schedel, *Liber Chronicarum*, Nuremberg, 1493 (Rogers Fund, 1906).

The illustration on page 111 is a detail from a woodcut in *Terentius der hochgelert*, Strasbourg, 1499 (Harris Brisbane Dick Fund, 1926).

The princely banquet on page 124 is a woodcut by Michael Wolgemut in the *Schatzbehalter*, Nuremberg, 1491 (Rogers Fund, 1919).

Reproduced on the endpapers is a section of a fifteenth-century manuscript of the *Forme of Cury*, graciously lent for the exhibition "The Secular Spirit" at the Cloisters by Dr. Curt F. Bühler, Research Fellow Emeritus, The Pierpont Morgan Library.

Designed by Peter Oldenburg
Composed and printed by The Stinehour Press